MY POOR PLATES OF MEAT

Eating and Drinking my Way Along the Camino de Santiago

IAN PEARSON

© Ian Pearson 2022

Published by Ian Pearson
The Old Cider House, 25 Castle Street
Nether Stowey, Somerset TA5 1LN

www.mypoorplatesofmeat.co.uk

ISBN 978-0-9933573-4-3

All photographs © Ian Pearson

CONTENTS

PLATES OF MEAT

For those of you not familiar with Cockney rhyming slang, 'Plates of Meat' are 'Feet'

INTRODUCTION

Lynne and I were supposed to be walking the Great Wall.

I had never heard of Surtr. No one outside Iceland had heard of Surtr. Surtr the Swarthy was a local volcano demon and he was as mad as Björk[1] on a British TV chat show. In a fit of pique, he wielded his flaming sword and lopped off the icy top of Eyjafjallajökull with the ease of a retired major decapitating a soft-boiled egg, exposing its molten caldera to the gods above. Freyr the fertile, goddess of rain and sun and all things meteorological, sprinkled in her moist magic and Loki, the transgender and cunning trickster, shook it all up a bit. Imagine an adolescent's zit – and the mess on the bathroom mirror.

Eighteen hundred kilometres to the south I was about to board an Air China flight to Beijing. A half term Heathrow was buzzing with the eager anticipation of thousands of excitable children and the already evident despair of as many harassed parents. Children and parents who would, within a few hours, have their holiday dreams dashed by the jolly Tannoy announcement that all flights had been grounded.

It appears that volcanic ash travels very long distances. First it reaches a couple of kilometres into the atmosphere where Njörðr, the Norse god of the wind, takes over and distributes the fine ash hither and thither. The fine ash is, in fact: rock, mineral and glass particles. Aeroplane engines are not a lover of any of these, especially the glass which melts in the furnace of a modern 747's engine. There is a technical expression for this; 'gumming'. Gummed engines tend to breakdown and then the aeroplane falls out of the sky.

We went home.

With northern Europe skies now free of vapour trails, three weeks holiday planned, the dog being looked after and an 'out of office' pinging to clients, a Plan 'B' was required.

"Where can we go for three weeks without flying?" I pondered.

Boats.

Boats don't care about rock, minerals and glass and rarely fall out of the sky.

---

[1] Icelandic pop musician known for her eccentric interview style in the 1990s.

1

"Hello. Brittany Ferries? … Have you got a berth for two leaving to Spain any time soon?"

"Yes."

"When does it leave?"

"Three hours' time."

"Book it. We'll see you at Plymouth."

Some holidays take months to plan. Walking the Great Wall of China had taken months to plan. Jumping in the car, telephoning the insurance company to organise a green card, arranging breakdown cover and stopping off at W. H. Smiths[1] to buy the *Rough Guide* took less than three hours.

We stood at the sharp end; Lynne, arms extended, a coastal breeze ruffling her hair and the imagined, angelic, voice of Céline Dion[2] whispering of love and dreams. Santander steamed ever closer, its red roofed apartment blocks, golden beach and coastal ozone scent hinting of the exotic. We had arrived. I wondered if they took yuan[3].

First stop, Rioja.

Driving along the straight and, quite frankly, not very interesting Autovía A-12, we passed countless back packers, all heads down and determined to get somewhere. It was hot and dusty and there must have been more scenic routes … a sponsored walk, Duke of Edinburgh's[4] (or Spanish equivalent), army manoeuvres? A bar at Santo Domingo de la Calzada held the answer.

Pilgrims.

What I had thought to be the trunk road from Pamplona to Burgos was actually a thousand year old pilgrim route, the Camino de Santiago - the Way of Saint James. Rule one; never engage a pilgrim in conversation unless you have an hour or two to spare.

"Where have you walked from?" I enquired.

"France, 200 kilometres to the east."

"Where are you walking to?"

"Santiago, 600 kilometres to the west."

"And why have you stopped here?"

---

[1] UK bookstore and stationers. *Rough Guide*, British travel guide series.
[2] Céline Dion sang the title song to James Cameron's film, Titanic. Kate Winslet starred and the iconic still from the film had her standing at the bow of the ship.
[3] Chinese currency.
[4] Youth adventure and experience programme.

"Chickens."

I nodded sagely.

Back in the car, I said to Lynne "Do you fancy walking the Camino de Santiago?"

"No."

Minehead, west Somerset[1]. Four years later.

There's a joke about a tourist in Ireland who asks one of the locals for directions to Dublin. The Irishman replies: 'Well sir, if I were you, I wouldn't start from here'. If the joke had originated in England, then the tourist may well have been in Minehead asking for directions to Santiago, except here the Englishman says, "Well sir, you're in luck, this just happens to be the Camino Inglés."

Minehead is the start of many things: a stag weekend at Butlins, the West Somerset Railway, the South West Coast Path and, should you have been around half a millennium ago, an arduous and dangerous boat trip to the northwest tip of Spain.

Lynne and I strolled along the harbour front with two pasties and a sausage roll for the dog; all hot, eaten straight from the paper bag and, in the case of the Labrador, with the paper bag. Two giant hands held a bronze Ordnance Survey[2] map marking the start of the 1,000 kilometre South West Coast Path and, today we were to follow its route up over North Hill following the sea westwards.

"Lynne. Did you know this is also the start of the English Camino de Santiago? Fancy walking it some time?" I suggested.

"No."

Bristol Airport. Two years later.

There were no boats from Minehead - hadn't been for years. If you'd been around in the sixteenth century you could have sailed the world: Cork, Cardiff, La Rochelle. A century later, English privateers sailed around the coast to pillage Spanish and French ships and also in the mix, there were the pious Christians who were willing to risk their necks in the open sea off the Cornish coast and through the Bay of Biscay[3] in the name of pilgrimage.

---

[1] County in south west England.
[2] National mapping agency for Great Britain.
[3] Atlantic waters known for being treacherous.

No boat, but there was a bus, a steam train, a bus, a diesel train, a bus and finally, cattle class on a budget airline to Bordeaux.

"Lynne. Are you looking forward to walking the Camino?"

"No."

FRANCE

The French were on strike today. They were on strike yesterday too. Yesterday the French air traffic controllers were on strike. Today, was the turn of SNCF, the state-run railway. As you can imagine, this was somewhat inconvenient if you wanted to travel to, or within, France. We wanted to travel to, and within, France. It was somewhat inconvenient.

The French love a good strike, 'la grève', it's a national pastime. Named after the former Place de Grève in Paris, employed but grumpy workers would gather on the gravel to work out ingenious ways to make people's lives somewhat inconvenient.

Few things had changed. SNCF had come up with a new type of alternating strike this year; ten out of ten for ingenuity. Workers would strike on two days out of five for three months. They had websites and everything, with days clearly marked when the trains would not be running. Inconvenience clearly articulated at the click of a mouse.

SNCF's website said '*If a TGV is marked as available to book (until the 16th of June), even on a strike day, then it is sure it will run as planned. You can purchase these tickets without worry.*'

We didn't worry. We purchased our tickets. The train didn't run.

And, the reason for the strike? President Macron, elected on a ticket to reform French industry, is attempting to reform French industry and bring it into the twenty-first century. Even bringing it into the twentieth century would be a start. The unions were a little 'fromaged off' about this. This is the thing about the French, they love the concept of radical change, give their leaders a mandate to do so and then don yellow jackets and throw stones at them if they try to implement the said reforms.

SNCF workers are gods. New recruits, from long lines of SNCF families, full of heroic tales of their forefathers inconveniencing passengers for each and every year since 1947, dreamt of sitting idly around red hot braziers, warming their hands and handing out leaflets explaining how hard done by they were.

Guaranteed job for life, free travel, retirement at fifty and only having to work three days out of five when there's a strike on and still getting paid. What's not to like?

Whilst the drivers were on strike the public relations people were doing a sterling job, setting up temporary advice tents with hot coffee and neat, pleated skirted staff armed with revised timetables. It was very professional. They'd had a lot of practice.

"We need to get to Bayonne" said I. The neatly turned out women consulted their revised timetables, offered coffee and then told us it would be "impossible" (with emphasis on the 'eee' bit in the middle) although, give them their due, they were very helpful in doing so. As an afterthought they suggested we went to the ticket office to ask for a refund. I didn't know this was some sort of ironic Gallic joke.

The ticket office wasn't open. Why bother opening? There was a strike on you know.

It was Helmuth von Moltke the Elder who coined the phrase 'No battle plan ever survives contact with the enemy'. This was war; the enemy? SNCF. We needed a Plan B… and coffee.

Last night's hotel had coffee, and breakfast, and Wi-Fi so we slunk back. The receptionist who checked us out greeted us.

"No trains?"

"No"

"There's a bus, but it'll be busy. There might not be any tickets left."

"Thank you."

Fortified with non-SNCF coffee (we weren't going to give them the pleasure of thinking they were in any way being helpful and assisting us) and with the wonders of the Internet we secured two rocking horse poo[1] tickets on the one o'clock bus. Job done. Well, some of the job done as we still needed to get from Bayonne to St Jean Pied de Port, but we'd cross that (railway) bridge if, and when, we got to it.

Perhaps the ticket office would be open back at the station? It was. There was a queue.

---

[1] Something exceedingly rare or, more likely, non-existent.

Getting to see one of the nice ladies in the ticket office involved obtaining a ticket from a little machine – the correct ticket for the type of service you wanted. We wanted the refund window. Everyone wanted the refund window. There was no ticket for a refund. We collected a ticket for buying a ticket for a non-running train and waited for our turn.

"May we have a refund please?" I said in my best French to the lady on the other side of the plexiglass.

"Oui" came the response. I handed over my e-ticket. "Ah non" followed by an apology along the lines of the fact that I had bought the ticket through an agency and would need to go through the same agency to get a refund. The fact that SNCF's website secretly makes everyone from the UK buy though an agency meant that we were not going to get a refund that day, so we walked off to find something else to do for the next four hours on a wet and windy Monday morning.

Bordeaux may be the capital of wine but today it was like any other provincial city; drab and grey except a bit more French. We got soaked at the Place de la Bourse, were unimpressed by the Miroir d'Eau (Water Mirror) as it was hissing down already and the effect was lost on us and we saw the Grosse Cloche, and it did what it said on the tin – it was a big bell. The Saint-André Cathedral was, at least, dry inside and we admired the enormous organ (a must see according to the guide), before giving up on outside (and inside) attractions and settling into a café for more coffee. I very much hoped the bus had a toilet on board.

Buses are the poor cousin in the family of French modes of transport and as such are hidden away out of sight and mind on the outskirts of the city, like some mad and smelly uncle. We followed the signs to the bus station only to find that the bus stop was, in fact a piece of waste ground that looked suspiciously like an abandoned gypsy encampment with jettisoned tyres and feral dogs roaming about. The only reason we knew that it was a bus stop was the fact that other equally lost train passengers, were waiting with bags and suitcases in the hope that a bus would turn up.

I consulted an inadequate map and timetable to see where the bus would stop. The map had almost disappeared under a dirty crater of a thousand fingers trying to get their bearings and the faded timetable was out of date by two years. No clues; this was France.

The buses all entered at the same place. In a lightbulb moment of resourcefulness, I told Lynne that I would wait at the entrance and identify the bus as it arrived. Genius. Or it would have been if all the buses hadn't had 'Bordeaux' written on the front of them. Back to the drawing board of continually running to wherever a bus stopped to wait patiently for the driver to enter the next destination into his little handheld keyboard.

A very green and orange bus did turn up, the driver typed into his little keyboard and the words Bayonne dot matrixed above the front windscreen. A hoard of people surged forward forming what could loosely be called a scrum, but which the French believed was a queue, and we waited patiently (well, we British did) while the bus driver haphazardly chose people to process. At our randomly designated time, I produced our e-ticket on my phone which the driver read on his phone (which miraculously worked) and we settled in for our three hour journey south towards our destination.

My preferred reading for the journey was a book by Connor O'Donoghue called '*Overweight, Undertrained and Terrified: A Camino Diary*'. Connor was morbidly obese, gay and vastly underprepared. I'm not sure why I chose this book. Perhaps it was the fact that if this bloke could do it, then so could I.

I'm not sure of the word that describes an act so poorly performed or executed as to be held up as an example of how not to do something. Whatever, this was that book. Whatever Connor did, I would do the opposite.

We arrived at a building site. Bayonne was being dug up. Not bits of it, not in some orderly fashion – no; all of it, all at the same time. It was city planning on an amphetamine high and it was chaos.

The bus air-braked to a juddering halt outside the railway station. A railway station with no trains as the helpful station official informed us. But there was a replacement bus service to St Jean Pied de Port with a bus at six o'clock.

So, we had two hours to kill in the shambles that was Bayonne. Perhaps it looked lovely once, with its children's paint box shuttered apartments abutting the river but, today, it looked as if the Luftwaffe had just carpet bombed the place.

Two hours is just enough time to find a bar, write a couple of postcards and finish Connor's account of his trip. I felt for the man. If I had read the book prior to planning this trip, I probably wouldn't have started.

The replacement bus service arrived. The driver was smiley. The driver was on overtime. There was a lot of overtime for bus drivers during the SNCF strike. And he needn't worry, it would be his turn to be on strike in a month or so's time. It's not just planes and trains that can be inconvenient.

Construction site gave way to suburbs which, in turn, became open countryside. Wherever we were going, it was going to be up as gravity pushed us back into our seats. We passed though Alpinesque villages with their white walled chalet residences and the further and higher we went, the more affluent the properties became. I thought I caught the faint melodic voice of Heidi[1] wafting down from the mountains that lay ahead of us.

We arrived at the station in the last rays of the setting sun, retrieved our worldly possessions for the next couple of months from the cavernous underbelly of the bus and struggled awkwardly to place them on our backs. Sheeplike, we all followed the most confident looking backpack into town.

Tumbleweeds blew through St Jean Pied de Port. Where were the hordes of joyous pilgrims singing *Kumbaya*, bars bursting at the seams with young backpackers, restaurants giving away victuals to the sandaled poor?

The town was like a Sunday afternoon in Letchworth[2] as we walked in an eerie silence up to the Pilgrims' Office (Acceuil Pelerin). And the reason? Well, many of you may think the purpose of the Camino is the challenge of walking 800 kilometres, gaining spiritual enlightenment or becoming at one with nature. But you'd be wrong. The real reason to undertake this path is to collect stamps in a little

---

[1] Novel about a five year old girl living with her grandfather in the Swiss Alps.
[2] Unassuming town to the north west of London.

passport or '*credential*'. This is the ultimate boys' (and girls') sticker book albeit without the playground swaps.

A friendly man beckoned us in as we poked our heads around the door.

"Come in." he said.

How did he know we were English? Did we look English? Perhaps English was to be the lingua franca of the route. I very much hoped so.

We availed ourselves of a couple of lime green village hall chairs. Opening the desk drawer, the man withdrew a stack of folded cards, withdrew two and placed them with care and reverence in front of us. With OCD[1] precision he inked a wooden handled stamp and with a

practiced eye set the stamp perfectly in the centre of the first empty square. He then waited, an expectant smile gracing his face. Was there something we'd forgotten? Of course - we needed to have our photograph taken holding the card. I struck what I thought was an appropriate pose: part heroic, part determined, part 1960s men's cardigan knitting pattern model. 'Click' went the fabricated sound effect of our mobile phone. Job done.

"Would you like a shell?"

We were prepared for this. The scallop shell has been carried by pilgrims since time immemorial and appears on signs, logos and merchandise all along the route. Pilgrims with no other possessions would have drunk from it and the monks along the route would have filled it with food, just enough to keep body and soul together, never too much to suggest greed or gluttony.

---

[1] Obsessive Compulsive Disorder.

The shell also had a symbolic meaning with each of the splayed spines on the shell representing the different routes taken by pilgrims all converging on Santiago de Compostela.

Delving into my rucksack, and with a 'hey presto', I produced my own shell, brought all the way from the UK and repurposed for the trip. Its original purpose was that of a coquille St Jacques from Marks and Spencer[1] with two neat holes drilled into it ready for its journey tied to the back of my rucksack.

Grasping my pristine credential, I thanked the kindly volunteer. This was my passport to the Camino. It gave me my purpose, an introduction to my sleeping quarters and cheap food. Its value would increase with every sello (stamp) and we would need one of these every day and at every overnight stop to prove that we hadn't bunked off or cheated in any way. There had to be a black market in these.

We had a private apartment booked and after a 30 second shower were ready to hit the town. Most places were closed, well it was the first weekend of the 'season', but the Café Ttipia looked warm and welcoming. The door swung open into the womblike bar and it was obvious that we were going to get communal from the get go with long benches of pilgrims already sitting chatting and drinking. Adopting a slightly lost and 'please adopt me' countenance we were soon waved over, bench seats patted, bottoms shuffled and beers passed from pilgrim to pilgrim until reaching their correct destination. We were now a family. We were also ravenous.

When in the Basque country, do as the Basques do. The Basques like hearty casseroles and the plat de soir (set evening meal) was stewed neck of lamb with tiny carrots, broad beans and red peppers. Queso Idiazabal, a goats' cheese made locally gave the accompanying risotto a creamy gorgeousness, its smoky tang infused from the cheese drying in the chimney of the producer's wood fired farmhouse. With food like this we would have to walk 20 kilometres every day, if only to stop us turning into Mr Creosote[2]. Add to this the pokey 14% rustic red and we could not have hoped for a better start to our adventure.

---

[1] Upmarket British food and clothing retailer.
[2] A very obese character from Monty Python's film *The Meaning of Life*.

ST JEAN PIED DE PORT – PAMPLONA

Brass monkeys[1] was what it was. Whatever heating system the apartment had was not going to bother to turn on for ten minutes while a couple of itinerant pilgrims quickly donned their walking apparel. Warming up was required and, being British, there was only one option. Tea. None of that foreign yellow Lipton stuff mind you, a proper piano playing chimp brew[2] was required and we had brought a supply.

And now a question; what route to take?

There were a couple of routes into Spain and we had a preferred route, a rough and rugged hike over barren mountainous terrain. This was known as the 'Route Napoleon'.

Napoleon, not necessarily known for his leisure hiking, had forged a path through the Pyrenees from this very point. He hadn't been the first, the Romans had been there and done that donkey's years before. Invading armies liked the route as it was open with good visibility meaning attackers could be seen from miles away. The only downside was that open and high also meant cold and prone to atrocious weather.

The kindly volunteer from last night said it would snow. Napoleon was a hard military type and used to a bit of trudging. Lynne and I were not. Kindly volunteer suggested the soft military leader route, the way of Charlemagne (don't tell him I called him soft). So, we decided to walk in the slippers of Charles the Great, Emperor of the Romans, King of the Franks.

Read anything about how to walk the Camino and everything points to the crack of dawn as being a good time to start. Long, gruelling days were going to be the order of the day and the sooner we set off the more kilometres (or miles for those of a more British disposition) we could get under our belts. This was not such an issue for us as we were starting off in April, but for the majority of pilgrims,

---

[1] A colloquial expression taken from 'cold enough to freeze the balls off a brass monkey'. These were tourist souvenirs from the Far East.
[2] PG Tips tea was advertised on television using chimpanzees. One advert had a chimp, Mr Shifter, playing the piano: [Son] "Dad, do you know the piano's on my foot?" [Father] "You hum it son, I'll play it!"

commencing their walk in the summer months, walking at midday was not an option. Spain can get awfully hot.

There was, however, perhaps a more pressing reason for starting off early; pilgrims wanted the best bunks in the albergues. For 'best' read 'cheapest' as often pilgrims are on a tight budget and the best value accommodation can go very quickly. We did not anticipate this being a problem. We were not going to have the competition for bed spaces that the later hordes would experience and we also had a credit card. We were a dangerous breed of pilgrim - pilgrims with money!

Whatever time we decided to start for the rest of the walk, today was going to be one of the longest and hardest of the entire trip so an early start was required. It was pitch dark when we got up and it was still so as we started off. We stood at the entrance to our accommodation and took a deep breath, a breath that fogged as we released it. It was still well below freezing.

Neil Armstrong scribbled down a few words with his $128.89 pencil before exiting Apollo 11 and took "a giant leap for mankind". Lao Tzu started his thousand miles with a single step. Ralph Waldo Emerson's life was a journey, not a destination. My turn:

"Lynne, are you looking forward to this?"

"No."

Street lights illuminated the way, the cobbled road glistening with frost. Nothing stirred and the moment was serene. Where were the pilgrims from last night? Did they not know that this was going to be a long day? Perhaps they had beaten us to it?

"Excuse me." a blonde haired woman called out. "I think I may be lost."

I looked around. In one direction was the town, still in darkness, in the other the shining beacon of the

Porte d'Espagne, bathed in sodium etherealness, the gateway to the Camino. I suggested that, perhaps, we should head toward the light and she willingly agreed.

At the gate we took turns to take each other's photos as had countless thousands of others since the dawn of photography starting on this momentous journey. Our new friend was from Denmark and had left her two children at home with their father to 'take the journey of a lifetime'. So much information in so little time.

We were soon at the crossing of paths and the choice of Napoleon or Charlemagne. This was our last chance. Would we brave the rugged open path favoured by the French emperor or would we wimp out and follow the path of the N-135 over the top like Charlemagne?

If we hadn't made our mind up by now, then perhaps the story of the poor Pyrenean pilgrim from centuries past would have helped us make the decision.

Back in the day, this Napoleonically inspired but hapless pilgrim decided to spend the night at an inn to shelter from the weather. He found his room but was soon awakened by another pilgrim entering. Given that the road was dangerous and two people were safer from bandits than both travelling alone, the pilgrims hooked up. Bad choice. The second pilgrim was none other than one of the feared bandits and he stabbed the man and made off with his possessions. Bleeding to death, a pack of wolves circled but were kept at bay by, guess who? Saint James. Thinking he had got away with the murder, the bandit stopped for a rest, only to be eaten by the said wolves again led by the apostle Santiago.

Charlemagne it was to be.

'The first day's the hardest' suggested everything we had read. What did they know? Gently rolling pastureland, cows nonchalantly chewing the cud, light cotton wool clouds scudding across the sky. This was a walk in the park.

The guidebooks and blogs about the Camino spoke of quaint roadside cafés, itinerant orange sellers, spontaneous acts of generosity from locals bearing cups of coffee. So far, we had seen nothing save for a few bovines that were giving up their milk for no one. We were getting hungry and thirsty. Hamlets came and went. If there was a café

15

then the local shutter maker had got there first. A Ukrainian couple that we'd got into stride with were getting worried. We walked with them for a while passing one darkened café after another. We broke into our emergency rations. We shared our chewy bars with them. They wouldn't die.

The gentle ambling road had taken on a somewhat more vertiginous course with stony paths replacing the easy to navigate metalled road – we were in the foothills of the Pyrenees and the only way was up.

Mid morning came and went and then we came across a bar. An open bar.

The bar was buzzing. Pilgrims poured in to join the locals who appeared to have been ensconced for quite some time, probably since a very liquid breakfast looking at some of them. I queued in line at the counter.

"Deux baguettes de porc s'il vous plait." Blank look. "Two pork baguettes please." Blank look. Never mind. Point, make pig noise, mime eating. An employer of mine once spent thousands of pounds for me to take a Chamber of Commerce business French course. How disappointed they would have been to know that I couldn't even order a sandwich.

A group of French farmers, after a full day's work applying for EU[1] subsidies, sat at a corner table eating their hearty meat based meal. It was eleven o'clock and they had already demolished a bottle of red wine each and were tucking into their second. No further grant applications would be forthcoming that day. All they now had to do was drive their tractors very slowly along single track roads to hold up some traffic. It's a hard life.

Our calves had started to feel the ascent prior to the rest break and they would be stretched further for the next 14 kilometres. It started to rain and we donned waterproofs as the previously springlike weather was now turning decidedly wintery. The further up we went up the whiter the rain got. Soon the white started sticking to the ground.

---

[1] The European Union.

Layering was my strategy for climate control on this walk and I progressively donned each layer, piece by piece, getting progressively more rotund. My rucksack was now remarkably light which was a blessing. Michelin-menlike we plodded on, the kilometres subject to some Einsteinian theory of relativity whereby the steepness of the climb and the volume of the snow made the length of the route expand exponentially.

After what seemed to be ten or so kilometres, we had walked two. At this rate we wouldn't reach our accommodation until after dark and walking in the dark, in the snow, over the Pyrenees was never going to be a good idea. We needed to step up a pace. Perhaps a few rounds of 'Valderi-Valdera'[1] would raise the spirits. This was a stupid idea. Certain songs become earworms. If the song is a rock classic then this shouldn't be a problem. However, hour after hour of the *Happy Wanderer* going round in one's head will drive you insane.

The route was relentless, but at least we were hugging the road rather than the open landscape of Monsieur Napoleon's followers and the path was good, if long and winding. We would not get lost. Flurries became showers. Showers became squalls. Squalls became a blizzard. I later found out that the road appears on www.dangerousroads.org and I could see why as it snaked and zig-zagged up, hugging the side of the steep mountains.

Despite the inclemency of the weather our pace quickened, possibly as a consequence of trying to fend off hypothermia. We saw few others, mainly because we had the hood of our waterproofs tightly secured around our faces and our heads down to avoid the worst of the biting wind and snow. This would also have been the reason that we did not notice the 'Welcome to Spain' sign that we must have passed.

Suddenly the snow stopped and we were forced to squint in blistering white light. It was still freezing but we had climbed out of the cloud into the High Pyrenees, surrounded by the snow covered tops of even higher peaks. The scene was almost celestial and after trudging for kilometre after kilometre in such abysmal visibility it was as if we could see again.

---

[1] From the *Happy Wanderer*. Florenz Friedrich Sigismund and Friedrich-Wilhelm Möller.

To add to the spirituality of the occasion we strode towards the edifice of a modern chapel, its roof jutting out like a nun's starched wimple. In front of it was a stone monument dedicated to Roland, the great mate of Charlemagne. This was Puerto de Ibañeta.

Charlemagne lived around the late eighth and early ninth centuries and was King of a loose grouping of Germanic tribes from the lower and middle Rhine region. These tribes had successfully conquered the north west region of continental Europe. Hence 'France' from the Franks.

Roland was a military commander under Charlemagne and it was at the Battle of Roncevaux Pass in 778, the spot where we now stood, that Roland was killed. His death may have passed as a postscript in the forgotten annals of history had it not been immortalised, and romanticised, in French literature as an epic poem. The *Song of Roland* has four thousand lines and was a 'chanson de geste' – a song of heroic deeds. For an excellent example of this style of poetry it is difficult to beat the *Brave Sir Robin* song from *Monty Python's Holy Grail* although it is unlikely that Roland '*when danger reared its ugly head, he bravely turned his tail and fled*' as did Sir Robin.

From this highest point of our journey the rest would be mercifully downhill. We stopped long enough to take a quick snap before taking a wide track back down into the clouds. We could endure a couple of kilometres of poor weather in the knowledge that we would be warm and dry within the hour.

Colditz Castle[1], or what very much looked like it, loomed out of the mist. Teutonic towers, whitewashed walls and small black windows greeted us as the terrain levelled. I thought I'd caught sweep of a searchlight … perhaps I was hallucinating. Here was our accommodation. Hopefully, I

---

[1] A German prisoner of war camp in World War II.

wouldn't need the file baked into my Red Cross Dundee cake.

'The first day's the hardest'. Okay, I get it now.

"Lynne, did you enjoy that?"

"No."

The Monasterio de Roncesvalles (pronounced ron-ce-buy-ayes) is the go-to B&B. Apart from looking like a prisoner of war camp it was to be our first albergue.

Albergues are hostels (hostals), monasteries, hospitals and refuges along the Camino catering for the needs of pilgrims. Some, like our present location, are large prestigious buildings catering for hundreds of people. Others may be just a room or two with a few bunk beds. Some charge, many do not and ask for a 'donativo' (donation) being what one can afford (if anything).

Albergue etiquette was a bit of a mystery. The guidebooks and blog sites talk about it endlessly. Suffice it to say the general gist is to try and not cheese off your fellow pilgrims OR the people that run these places. Rule One is that boots do not go into dormitories. We entered and immediately de-booted, stacking our sodden footwear onto drying racks with hundreds of other identical pairs. We had presence of mind to write our initials on the back heels of our boots. No one else had. Others would be very confused and disappointed in the morning.

Whilst we were albergue virgins, we were wise and had pre-booked our beds and meals in advance. That would save us time. We then joined the less wise virgins in exactly the same queue. The corridor was long and draughty. The Dutch volunteers were efficient, but there were a lot of us and most had not booked beds and meals in advance. What the place needed was an express checkout so that the prepared could gloat over the rest.

Apart from the wisdom of the virgins, the group queuing also fell into two other categories: the softie Charlemagnes and the mountain rescued Napoleons.

"It was the worst weather I've ever walked in." a young German sobbed. "People were turning around and many had to be rescued." Even as we discussed the weather, two pilgrims were brought in by medics with the early stages of hypothermia. Most had to turn around and take the 'walk in the park' route that we had walked adding another ten kilometres to an already long and gruelling day. Others returned to base. One pilgrim had decided to give up all together. "It is too hard" she said.

At the front of the queue, we dutifully handed over our pilgrim passports and marvelled at the stamp, now a badge of honour for having survived the first day. The nice Dutchman handed over our pre-paid dormitory tickets and a couple of vouchers for our evening meal to be taken in one of the two village restaurants. After yesterday's gourmet feast, we had high hopes.

IKEA[1] had undertaken the interior design of the dormitory, light beech the order of the day. Bunks were in groups of four and our bunk-mates for the night were two middle aged, middle classed Spaniards. We "hola'd" each other and set to peel off the sodden rags that had once been state of the art Gore-Tex walking gear.

"To the bar." was my rallying cry as Lynne and I set off to get soaked again as we ran the hundred or so metres to the café. A pile of rucksacks and equally sopping jackets hung by the door and the atmosphere had a plastic/sauna/sweat aroma to it. Two of their largest beers disappeared within seconds along with a couple of packets of jamón (ham) flavoured crisps for which I had developed an enormous craving. It was the salt I needed and I sucked each crisp of its (probably) unhealthy coating of flavourings.

"Dos cervezas más por favor." And two more beers (and crisps) arrived. These we could savour. My hands and feet were slowly regaining some feeling although that feeling was of electrifying pins and needles. I blew into my hands and the woman next to us said she had been there an hour and was still shivering. This is obviously what 'chilled to the bone' meant.

For entertainment we watched a young couple (early thirties, rich, spoilt, few social graces) arrive, perfectly dressed, and obviously hadn't just walked over the Pyrenees. The man left but the woman asked if the café had a room for the night and that she would like to see the room before deciding whether she would take it.

---

[1] Swedish furniture store.

Roncesvalles is not awash with a choice of accommodation and all of it caters for the pilgrim trade. Seven star comfort is not an option. Most bunk up with 70 other smelly, noisy co-pilgrims communally.

"It is not good enough." The woman told the hotelier and the rest of the bar in a loud voice. "Myself and my boyfriend must have a double bed". This confirmed to the ensembled pilgrims that they had not walked from St Jean. Had they done so, they would have been too tired for any form of night time intimacy. The woman stormed out.

Fifteen minutes later she reappeared to say that on reflection she would take the room and paid for it. At practically the same moment, and with Brian Rix-like[1] timing, the boyfriend reappeared to say that he had found, and booked, a better room somewhere else. The woman, without an ounce (gram?) of remorse told the proprietor that she had found somewhere better and wanted to cancel the room. The proprietor took back the key and when the woman asked for a refund, the proprietor told the woman that the credit card machine had inexplicably and inconveniently broken down in the last 15 seconds and she was unable to make a refund. A small cheer and round of applause went around the bar as the awful woman and her equally awful boyfriend left the bar, 60 euros out of pocket.

We finished our drinks and ran back to our dormitory in the continuous rain. Our waterproofs, state of the art as they were, were no match for the Pyrenean weather and through some sort of reverse osmosis process were now actively sucking in the rain. Whatever, we couldn't get any wetter.

Back at base we decided to lay down, just for five minutes, snug in our brand new coffin shaped sleeping bags. If we died, and given the day that we'd had this was not entirely out of the question, they were the right shape for burying us in. We snored like the rest of the room for an hour or so.

Turning the handle on the shower to the far right meant water hot enough to make tea, so I brewed myself for five minutes. We'd wrapped everything in polythene in our rucksacks and miraculously our second set of clothes were clean and dry. I felt nearly human again.

---

[1] English actor-manager, who produced long-running farces for the London stage. Scenes often had characters running on and off stage, narrowly missing each other.

Unfortunately, this feeling was only fleeting as we had to put on our rain-magnet waterproofs back on to run to the second hostelry boasted by the village, the Posada de Roncesvalles.

A roaring log burner welcomed us and laughter filled the air. We met our Danish friend turning the wrong way out of the toilet. She had been sitting with a new group of co-pilgrims who appeared to be drinking what looked like buckets of Spanish brandy. These were not their first buckets either. Lynne and I stuck to beer.

We chatted to the pilgrims around us; the Napoleons with the best survival stories, the Charlemagnes smug. Everyone proffered their name. Everyone else forgot it immediately. Nicknames replaced them and were remembered. One of this group became known to us as the 'Perky Australian'.

Some people we met were reserved, some to the extent that they never spoke or made eye contact. Others were annoyingly over the top. The Perky Australian was one of the latter. Within five minutes we knew he was a teacher, taught music, had a motorbike, travelled here, there and everywhere … and here he was in the bar with us with the distinct possibility that he would be dining with us at the eight-thirty sitting.

Fortunately, we were back in the lunchtime café for dinner and ran over for our first ever 'pilgrim menu'. Practically every eating establishment along the route had a pilgrim menu, even the poshest of places. These are usually three course meals with bread and wine at ridiculously low prices. Most menus were between eight and twelve euros. We'd heard that some were fantastic value for money others not quite so. We were just about to experience one of the 'not quite so' variety.

We sat at a table with a quiet Spaniard, Eduardo from Valencia. Luckily Eduardo's English was better than our Spanish and we soon got deep into conversation about the Camino, Spain, Brexit[1] and numerous other topics that rapidly became a blur as we waded our way through a second bottle of plonk. Whilst the company was lovely, the food was basic: cold macaroni in a tomato sauce, fried chicken quarter

---

[1] The withdrawal of the United Kingdom from the European Union.

with chips and a red coloured yoghurt. We would have to work on the food.

The albergues have a strict nightly curfew, usually ten pm. We managed to get in a with a few minutes to spare. Logs never slept so well.

The Spanish way of life is uniquely out of kilter with most other European countries. Your average Spaniard is not known for early mornings, loves a long lunch, perhaps a siesta in the afternoon and then a drink and a bit of tapas before a very late dinner. Camino life was not that of an average Spaniard.

Coughings, splutterings and murmured conversations were our alarm clock. It was six o'clock. Our Spanish bunkmates were up and raring to go as Lynne and I woke up, bleary eyed and not very raring. Lynne had managed to pull something in her groin, and not in a nice way, and was therefore taking it carefully as we dressed ready for Day Two of our trek.

I thought how, my now dry, waterproofs were going to fare today as I looked out of the window with my new Spanish bunk mate. I pulled a phrase from the very depths of my very poor Spanish, "Está lloviendo a cántaros" I said – "it's raining cats and dogs". My Spanish friend nodded sadly in agreement.

It was now the breakfast part of the dinner, bed and breakfast package from the albergue. Having experienced the dinner, we did not have high expectations of the breakfast. My expectations were met. One piece of toast, butter and jam washed down with a coffee. It was sufficient but I made a note to spend my three euros fifty more wisely in the future.

'Santiago de Compostela 790km' stated the road sign just outside the albergue. There was a queue of pilgrims having their photos taken beside it. It was obligatory.

"It's a bloody long way" says I. "Lynne, are you ready for this?"
"No."

It was still raining cats and dogs.

The path was a stream so we walked along the road, dodging truck made tsunamis as vehicles sped by us. I was beginning to think that this was, perhaps, not my best idea ever. We had chosen April and May for the trip as it wouldn't be too hot. Well, it certainly wasn't too hot, it was freezing.

The Perky Australian caught up with us although the driving sleet dampened even his enthusiasm and we trudged onwards, heads down in silence. My guidebook stated at one point, '*At the far end, ford a small stream ...*' The small stream turned out to be a fully formed river in full spate and so we detoured to cross at the nearest bridge.

A large pile of rucksacks greeted us as we entered the café at Espinal. The room was thick with the mist of tens of walkers drying gloves and hats on the school hall radiators, all cast iron and black. Coffees and custard pastries were the order of the day. Lynne washed down a couple of ibuprofen. Day Two and she was already a cripple.

No one relished the idea of reapplying their soggy outer garments but kilometres needed walking and arms were threaded with difficulty into non compliant sleeves and boots squelched as equally wet socks were placed into them. If we survived this week without trench foot it would be a miracle. The cat and dogs were splashing in the puddles as we left. If anything, it was raining harder.

The next village, Viscarreta, had a number of inviting bars. We tossed a coin. Should we have an early lunch or plough on? Tails dictated that we would press on ahead and get to our overnight stop at Zubiri. Next time we would make more informed decisions.

My diary entry for the day underlined the word 'long' when describing the journey. Every kilometre felt like three as we dragged litres of water in our clothing with every step. A steep limestone path, smooth like marble, was our route into the village. The torrential rain, formed a river ready to sweep our feet from under us at every footfall. I kept promising Lynne that we were "nearly there". She'd had enough. She didn't believe me.

A lone Englishman joined us. At least we had someone to talk to and to take our minds off the treacherousness of the path. He was debating where to stay that night. I consulted the guidebook and told him that it suggested Larrasoaña (the next village) as Zubiri was an *'uninspiring industrial town'* and that *'pressing on was a worthwhile option'*. He thanked us for our sage advice and strode onwards.

Mentions of 'the guidebook' refer to *A Pilgrim's Guide to the Camino de Santiago* by John Brierley, usually referred to as 'the Brierley'. Its tagline was, *A Practical and Mystical Manual for the Modern-Day Pilgrim*. It contains detailed maps, a history of the route, language tips, directions, heights and elevations and places to stay. It is a very comprehensive guide and invaluable. It also contains Mr Brierley's thoughts on many things, including: the *'practical path'*, the *'mystical path'* and *'personal reflections'*.

The practical path is, on the whole, a brief description of what that part of the route holds. The mystical path is a dreamy otherworld encounter with the route with far too many references to God, prayer and spirituality (in my opinion). The personal reflections build upon the mystical bit and are in italics, no doubt to separate fact from fiction. Luckily, the last two sections (mystical and reflections) are in purple making them very easy to spot and skip over.

The Puente de la Rabia, an old medieval bridge, took us into the centre of our night-time destination. The river level was alarmingly high and our B&B for the night extremely close to the river. We needn't have worried. The house had stood there since the seventeenth century with walls that Charlemagne would have found difficult to breach.

We were staying in a 'casa rural' meaning country house. These could be self-catering or, in our case, serviced accommodation. The owners had beautifully restored every detail of this building with highly polished dark wood, wobbly floors and rough stone throughout. It was also warm and cosy. We thought of those poor souls in the municipal albergue – but not for very long.

We decided to explore the town. Whatever Brierley said, it must have some redeeming features; a Romanesque church or interesting statue or something. However, as we left the casa we found we were next door to the Bar Valentine which was playing soft, enticing jazz; well, we could always explore tomorrow morning. Beers and a couple of open tuna sandwiches made us feel half human again rather than the drowned rats that had we'd been half an hour previously.

They call it 'sleep inertia'. It's that awful feeling you get when you wake up after a mid-afternoon sleep and feel like death warmed up. I felt like death warmed up. Supposedly there's an art to having a siesta. Firstly, it takes practice. This would not be a problem, we'd seven weeks to get into the swing of it. Secondly, don't sleep too long. NASA found that 26 minutes was the perfect length. Next, follow Winston Churchill's example and have a strong espresso before going to sleep. None of the above included having beers and a tuna sandwich.

We decided to take a walk before dinner to cure our sleep inertia. Zubiri didn't take long to explore. Its main attraction was the bridge that we'd crossed on the way in. Legend had it that a rabid animal could be cured by leading it though the central arch of the bridge three times. Perhaps Lynne's groin strain could be cured by traipsing her round the arch thrice? Perhaps not.

The restaurant heaved with pilgrim customers, all as knackered as we were. Many had limps, blisters, strains, sprains and the few shops in town all sold bandages, supports, sticks and pain relief. I took my pain relief in the form of beer.

Two beers arrived. Identical glasses yet one contained about 25 centilitres the other overflowing past the half litre mark. I wondered if they had weights and measures and a trading standards department at the local council? I drank the big one and ordered another.

Once bitten, twice shy. We avoided the pilgrim menu and went for the selection of croquetas, all potato based and deep fried. The mushroom and blue cheese variety was pure comfort food much needed after the day we'd had. A main dish of albondigas followed; the beef meatballs swimming in a rich and spicy tomato and garlic sauce, partnered by a local Tempranillo. Those partaking of the pilgrim menu looked on with undisguised envy. They would learn.

Daylight. I poked my head out of the bathroom window. I was not surprised to see it was still pouring down. The proprietor of the B&B said that it was the worst weather they'd had for thirty years.

I retraced my steps to take a couple of photos of the bridge. As I did so, a car on the left bank became inundated by the flood waters. It teetered at the edge of the torrent and I got off the bridge as a precaution. A fellow pilgrim swiftly hopped across the bridge towards me. He too had seen that the car was likely to smash into it.

"The path's been washed away." he said.

Another Plan B was needed and I stopped to pick up 'Limping Lynne' and the, now, three of us took the main road out of town.

At least it was easy walking. Well, comparatively easy walking; we had to put up with lorries careering by mere metres from the white line we were walking along. Many of them did hoot either in sympathy for our soggy plight or as a mark of respect for what we were doing, or perhaps they were just letting us know they were travelling at 80 kilometres an hour and to get out of their way. The magnesium carbonate factory we passed was an interesting but ultimately ugly blot on a landscape with many blots to its name. At least we avoided El Puente de los Bandidos on the main road. Legend has it that bandits would lie in wait for medieval pilgrims to cross the bridge there and then relieve them of their worldly goods.

Brierley suggested Larrasoaña for breakfast and we detoured off the main road in search of warm bocadillos and a cortado (small half coffee/half milk). The place was a ghost town. We bumped into the Englishman from yesterday. We stupidly asked him how his accommodation was the previous night.

"Bloody awful. Cold damp rooms, no hot water and lukewarm macaroni in tomato sauce for dinner". I changed the subject quickly.

The next Brierley recommendation was also closed. However, we needed to eat something. It was Day Three and we were now forced to dig into the bottom of our rucksacks for the remaining half of our emergency rations. We sat on the forlorn garden furniture of the closed café and chewed on a peanut protein bar. We would have to replenish our stock of rations at the next town. A duck and a cat joined us. We shared our breakfast with them. They were very grateful.

Pamplona was our destination and whilst using the road was the quickest route, we'd had enough of playing Russian roulette with 26 tonners and, four kilometres from the city, an opportunity presented itself to take a more rural approach to the last part of the day's walk; one that did not follow the swollen river.

The route was over a steep ridge and after so much flatness, the opportunity to hike up and get a bit breathless was very appealing. A route map was situated in a gravel carpark and we consulted this along with a couple of keen Christians, one American the other Canadian. The latter was the spitting image of Ned Flanders from the Simpsons cartoon series[1], complete with similar puerile catchphrases. We started walking with them, wheezing as we stepped up and up along the path.

"What a zip-a-dee-doo-dah view" said Ned as we reached the top. 'You've got to be kidding me' I thought. "It's a bit uppity-up-up isn't it?" I could have strangled the bloke.

Wood and scrubland were our companions for the last few kilometres and Ned Flanders was right, it was uppity-up-up. It was also tranquil after the constant roar of rubber on tarmac that we had experienced for the past 15 kilometres.

Graffiti adorned the concrete walls of random derelict buildings as we approached the city and, in the ruined shell of barn, a Norwegian handed out hot, strong coffee from a flask in little plastic cups. All those guidebooks were right, there were nice people giving up their time to support us pilgrims. I took a bar of chocolate from his little shop and over donated for his kindness.

After seeing very few people all day a horde appeared at the Puente de Arre, a bridge at the entrance to the city. This normally tranquil and picturesque picnic spot had been turned into a raging torrent of white water and spume, the arches of the bridge barely visible as the boiling waters of the river threatened to breach the road crossing. If it did, at least some of the horde would be taken with it. The church (Cofradia de la Trinidad) by the bridge provided us with a sello. However, this was no ordinary stamp as it was double sized and I wondered if using

---

[1] Dysfunctional US family sitcom.

two squares on my credential would somehow be cheating. I stamped it at any rate.

A coagulation (yes, it's the correct collective noun) of sopping wet pilgrims met at the main bridge into Pamplona. The signage had petered out and we were all now sheepdogless. We were the Perky Australian, the Ukrainian couple we had met on the first day and the poor Englishman from Larrasoaña who still didn't look like he trusted me after the Brierley incident.

"Look. There's the cathedral. Why don't we just head for that?" suggested Lynne. Nods all round. We started to cross the bridge.

A small, elderly, black clad woman clucked at us like an over protective broody hen.

"No, No. Sígueme, sígueme." Follow me, follow me.

We followed her like a string of ducklings, metaphors mixing by the minute. At a junction she pointed and then made the turning sign with the crook of her hand. Spanish directions were just within my grasp.

"Recto?"

"Si."

"Entonces la izquierda?"

"Si."

"Recto?"

"Si."

I thought I said "straight ahead, then left, then straight ahead."

"Si, si. Bueno, bueno."

I was very pleased with myself.

We all thanked the hen/duck lady and made our way down a side road. We picked up the signage, brilliant. And then we entered the Parque Fluvial. Perhaps the name should have given us a clue. The whole area, as far as the eye could see, was under a metre of water, like a huge boating lake, but without the boats. We turned around and traipsed back, looking out for the old woman lest we had to explain ourselves. We then crossed the bridge and headed for the cathedral as Lynne had originally suggested.

Think Pamplona, and bull running and Hemingway come into mind. I was keen to immerse myself in the first city of the Way. My stomach was also keen to be filled. The Calle San Nicolás was the ideal place to both immerse and feed.

I had pictured this scene countless times. Entering a dark wooded bar, sitting on the tall stool, pointing at the array of food. So accurate was my imagination that the tapas bar could have been named Déjà Vu. It had been 20 kilometres since the coffee at the B&B and the protein bar. Half a protein bar; I remembered feeding the cat and duck.

We sat at the bar. I pointed at various snacks tantalisingly close but behind a glass screen. I asked questions to which I would never understand the reply and drank the local beer on tap. However, I was not eating tapas. I was eating 'pinchos' or 'pintxos' in Basque; little open sandwiches speared with a cocktail stick. Eggs, mushrooms, cheese. This was the breakfast I had missed.

However, something was niggling at the back of my mind. I thought perhaps I could hear something in the distance and straining to identify it, it occurred to me that it wasn't something I could hear, but something I couldn't. It had stopped raining.

Two nights had been allocated for each of the cities along the route. We had plenty of time and it would have been a shame to have rushed the opportunity to properly soak up the atmosphere and Spanish nightlife. Most pilgrims, however, did not have this luxury and Brierley set a blistering daily target of around 25 kilometres per day allowing the whole route to be completed in 33 days, one day for each of Jesus Christ's life. Given that no one knows anything concrete about this individual, then it is pure conjecture as to how long he lived, but there we are. For those who want to have an even more religious experience, you could take off every Sunday and have an extra day in Santiago. This would give you 40 days. Of course, 40 days is just another way of saying 'a lot of'. So, read into that what you will.

Pamplona may be best known for bull running but it also had another reputation; one that was very close to my heart – it was a Mecca for craft beer. Being the owner of the UK's smallest commercial brewery, travels are an education opportunity not to be missed. The first bar we visited had 20 such opportunities.

Brewers love: alliteration, ambiguity, anapodoton, archaism, bathos, catachresis, cliché, malapropism, onomatopoeia, parody, puns, superlatives and sesquipedalianism[1] when it comes to naming beers. The Spanish understood this. *Hoptical Illusion* and *Basil is the New Orange IPA* kicked off the tasting - the second rather too Crabtree and Evelyn[2] for my taste. By the time we'd drunk *Liquid Fear* (8.7%) and *Imperial Nitro Crispy Stout* (11%) things had got a bit out of hand.

It may have been the *Ernest Hoppingway* that did it. Last night had turned into a blur of bars, beers and tapas and I was suffering. Last night was a Thursday and this was 'student night' with all establishments offering cheap deals. I vaguely remember tracing the route of the bulls and squeezing into progressively smaller and more local bars. Make sign for beer, point at things that looked interesting had been my approach all night. And it had been fantastic. I think.

The Vuelta del Castillo Park was full of fresh air but deep breaths were not going to be enough. What we really needed was a full English breakfast and the café serving huevos flamencas provided the Spanish alternative: chorizo, fried potatoes, tomatoes and baked eggs. When in Rome and all that.

Cured of our hangovers, we headed off to the Cathedral. It had a pilgrims' rate so we entered. I'm not keen about paying to go in churches but it was only a couple of euros and we needed a stamp for our passports. It had everything expected of a cathedral: high vaulted ceilings, ornate altary bits and little side rooms dedicated to various dead people. It also had a museum. I played at being a royal at the computer generated dressing up machine but the pink Wendy house with plastic grass seats brought back the hallucinatory qualities of some of last night's brews.

Had we been here in July, we could have taken part in the festival of Saint Fermin - the running of the bulls. What this unlucky chap and bulls have in common has been lost in the mists of time and only bits of him actually rest in Pamplona. The rest of him is in a box at Amiens (France) where truculent locals chopped his head off in AD 303 for some reason or other. Miracles attributed to Fermin included sweet smells coming from his grave, causing the melting of ice and snow

---

[1] The practice of using long, sometimes obscure, words in speech or writing. Look up the rest!
[2] Now on-line retailer selling fragranced personal products like soap and bubble bath.

31

and helping flowers to grow. Many non believers would probably attribute this to spring!

For those with an interest in health and safety, it is probably true to say that crowding the narrow streets with very drunk (mainly male) individuals and then letting bulls at them is not a particularly good idea. The European Agency for Health and Safety at Work officials,

armed with clipboards, would probably have apoplexy. Then again, we chase cheese down very steep hills[1].

It wasn't July and we were safe from the bulls. However, one enterprising shop had recreated one of the streets and had filled it with life-like models of the bovine brutes with which we could have our photos taken. Donning red scarves and rolled up newspapers, Lynne and I lay in various prone positions, pulled in stomachs to avoid horns eviscerating us and rolled foetally to escape stampeding hooves. Yes, a rolled-up copy of today's El País will protect you from a 600 kilo bull. This had to be the best couple of euros spent so far.

Where there are bulls, there would be Hemingway and he stood in bronze form at the end of the Café Iruña's counter. The south facing windows illuminated the airy bar with its colonial feel and tobacco-stained walls. We felt the 1920s all around us and nearly ordered a cocktail, but the hour was not yet upon us and we settled for a beer.

It was here, in 1925, that Hemingway wrote *The Sun Also Rises*, the story of wastrels, the privileged and some very damaged characters; all in the context of bull fighting. The First World War had taken its toll and these universally awful individuals had little regard for their own lives or those of others. Drunk, broke and bitter, the main protagonists dwell on the meaninglessness of their lives whilst

---

[1] Cooper's Hill Cheese-Rolling and Wake, Gloucester, England.

sponging off fawning hoteliers, abusing the locals and having meaningless sex with each other.

I pulled a paperback copy of the book from my rucksack and started to read. The word 'pretentious' comes to mind.

A whole afternoon and evening needed filling and there were still trendy bars to be visited. Hoppy pale ales, Belgian-style browns, spoon standing porters were all researched thoroughly. Lists of beers came in bible sized manuals, serving staff were quizzed and fellow drinkers met. Time for dinner.

With a 35 litre rucksack there is very little space for anything other than essentials. Yet, on occasion, a posh restaurant beckoned and required somewhat more formal attire. Here we would turn up in our least crumpled and stained clothing and hope that the establishment had a dark corner in which to hide us.

The Antonenea was one such place. Very upmarket. In fact, it was so upmarket that we couldn't find the entrance. This was a place for people in the know, not the hoi polloi with their shells and sandals.

The tasting menu was 40 euros. For 42 euros they offered the tasting menu and half a bottle of wine. We had low expectations of the four euro bottle. We sheepishly entered, smoothing down the front of our creased shirts, crossing arms over pasta sauce stains. A table for two was offered in direct sight of other (normal) people and menus provided.

They'd mispriced the wine. The chardonnay went well with the amuse-bouche of tartare of tuna and potato with a mayonnaise foam. This was going to a posh meal. Anywhere with 'foam' on the menu had to be classy.

Quail with mayonnaise in pitta bread, grilled artichokes with a soya foam (more foam), apple and seafood tartare with ginger and lime sauce and crab ravioli for starters. The artistry wasn't wasted on us. Time and effort had gone into this. The colossal T-bone was martyred on the flaming grill, seared black on the outside and red and bloody in the middle. The sibling red wine, a rich crianza, was spicy and tanniny, and the perfect accompaniment. Itd also alerted us to what a great deal the two euro offer had been.

Puddings were as elaborate as the starters; a café bon bon, decaffeinated Baileys coffee mousse, apple on a biscuit base with lime cream and cream cheese with a parmesan tuille. And to think that our fellow pilgrims were probably tucking into macaroni in tomato sauce.

We staggered back to our apartment

"I can't go on. It's too hard" Lynne sobbed. I presumed it was the wine speaking rather than the usual, rational Lynne.

"We've done the worst bit, the weather's improved and we're nearly there." I lied. "You're not enjoying this as much as I am, are you?"

"No."

PAMPLONA – LOGROÑO

It was the weekend and locals joined the throng of pilgrims in the city, shopping bags laden with ingredients for meals with family and friends. We exited the city via the Citadel, originally a 16th century fort but now more of a roundabout.

It was eight o'clock, perhaps a bit late for the distance we had to walk, but we still had plenty of time. The pilgrim rush hour tended to be between seven thirty and eight with the keen ones kicking off at sixish. The really early risers tended to be those that were undertaking the walk in Jesus' years (33) and needed to cover significant distances each day. They also tended to be the ones that were queuing outside the albergues at opening time. In fact, the early risers were a bit of a pain in the bottom in that they woke up pilgrims at ungodly hours (there's a paradox), so much so that some albergues had set an earliest leaving time with the doors locked until then.

A row of wind turbines, stark white against the clear blue sky, were where we were heading. Yes, the rain had left us and the sun was out.

The owner of the café at Zariquiegui was in the wrong job. His school careers' master must have spotted that being a miserable, cantankerous and obnoxious individual were hardly the qualities needed in the hospitality industry, yet here he was. Every request for coffee or a sandwich was met with incredulity that someone would disturb the serenity of his day. I ordered tortilla on the basis that it was on the counter and didn't have to be made up in the kitchen and thus anger him further.

Lynne and I ate our eggy potatoes in the sunshine and even rolled up our sleeves to take advantage of the warmth of the day. It was astounding that a few hours of sun had dispelled all memory of the first three days when the weather had been, quite frankly, atrocious. It had not been surprising to hear that some pilgrims had given up and, had we lived in Spain and been able to hop on a train, this option would have been quite attractive.

The Devil was a constant problem on the Camino and we were about to enter one of the hot spots for evil doings. Here, climbing in the Sierra del Perdón, one hapless pilgrim, failing to fill his goat's bladder with sufficient water was now dying of thirst. Old Nick turns up in the form of a handsome young pilgrim. The Devil offered the pilgrim fresh water if he would renounce his faith in God. The pilgrim refused. The Devil had a second go, this time asking the pilgrim to disown the Virgin Mary. Again, the pilgrim said no. So, the Devil tried his luck a third time, this time asking the pilgrim to denounce Saint James. The pilgrim gave the same answer and, as if by magic, the Devil disappeared in a puff of sulphurous smoke and in his place was St. James himself who guided the pilgrim to a spring and used his own scallop shell to water the parched and true pilgrim. The fountain was dry today.

The wrought iron silhouettes of the Alto del Perdón are iconic. Depicted are pilgrims throughout the ages, heads down, battling against the wind. Some are on foot others on the backs of donkeys, some caped in the classic Camino garb of cloak and cockle hat, others looking just like us with backpacks and beanies.

Cameras and phones were swapped and pilgrims stood next to their favourite cut-out. Lynne chose a donkey. Like Land's End or John O'Groats, a signpost pointed out far away locations; New York, 5,800km and Berlin 1,500km. However, we were only interested in the pointer to Santiago de Compostela at 550km.

Looking back, I could see Pamplona some 12 kilometres in the distance and on the other side of the ridge, the vast plain containing the villages that we would pass through on our way to that evening's destination, Puente la Reina.

On the way down we met up with Matt and his father. Matt had walked part of the path before but his father hadn't, and by the way the father was smoking and wheezing I wasn't sure he would walk it this time. Others were walking with family members and for many it was a rite of passage and great for bonding. I'm not sure Lynne and I were bonding but last night's wine infused despair had been diffused somewhat and Lynne was in a much more positive state of mind.

At Uterga the sun-drenched patio of Albergue Camino del Perdón called to us. "Stop for a beer" it said. Who could resist such a siren call?

At a steep concrete ramp, just a mile from Puente la Reina, we came upon a Peanuts[1] cartoon stall, decked out in lemon and lime colours and run by a pony-tailed, teenage, girl – a real live Lucy van Pelt. Instead of the five cents sign this limonada girl asked for a donation. We gave a euro apiece. How quaint, until we totted up how much this young entrepreneur was making each day. With, on average a hundred or so pilgrims passing each day, or forty odd thousand a year, this Lucy probably needed an accountant and paid VAT. We collected our green lemon shaped stamp and walked up the ramp into Obanos with its lop-sided church of John the Baptist. The church held the skull of Saint William (Guillaume) Duke of Aquitaine who killed his sister in an attack of fury when he learned of her decision to settle in Obanos, 'a hidden place far from palaces' and devote her life to helping the poor.

Racked with guilt (who wouldn't be) he renounced his title and lived a life of poverty and prayer. So, what fate befell this murderer? Belmarsh?[2] No, canonisation! On his named day the villagers drink claret imbibed through the saint's cranial remains. No, honestly – every Maundy Thursday the villagers drink the communion wine out of his head.

At the entrance to Puente la Reina we were greeted by a stylised bronze statue of St James with his broad felt hat and staff adorned with scallop shell. We were also greeted by the smell of sausages cooking on an outside barbecue. Lunch was required.

The Plaza Julián Mena with its arched porticoed square and cobbled pavement boasted a bar. Two very large Estrella Galicias were ordered and we found ourselves in conversation with the bar's friendly drunk, Carlos. As we were English, Carlos was keen to tell us

---

[1] American newspaper comic strip written and illustrated by Charles M. Schulz.
[2] His Majesty's Prison Belmarsh. Category-A men's prison in south-east London.

that he had fought in the Falklands War, on the Argentinian side. How to win friends and influence people!

We ordered local, home-grown asparagus and peppers garnished with a fried egg, courtesy of the owner who had picked them just that morning. To prove the point, he showed us his calloused hands, still encrusted with dirt. We hoped he had not prepared our food. We settled into a second pint, bathing in the warm spring sun and trying to ignore the heroic tales of Carlos and his Guerra del Atlántico Sur.

Our hotel was just around the corner and after the obligatory siesta and a shower we were ready to hit the town and see what Puente la Reina had to offer on a Saturday night.

Nothing.

There had to be some lively Latin quarter hidden amongst the maze of alleyways. What did the hordes of pilgrims do of an evening? It dawned on us that Puente la Reina didn't do nightlife. In fact, it didn't exactly do life.

The restaurant we chose was of the wooden platter variety, rather than the far more sensible 'put the food on a plate so that it doesn't roll off' type. The menu took a bit of translation and I had to resort to my Spanish dictionary for 'cuarto de gorrín asado' (a quarter of a sparrow). Perhaps this was taking nouvelle cuisine a little too far. In the end I plumped for the grilled duck breast with potatoes and peppers covered in a sprinkling of rock salt. A bottle of Sarria Crianza washed the meal down nicely. I later found out that 'gorrin' is, in fact, suckling pig. 'Gorrión' is sparrow. An easy mistake to make.

Tomorrow was Sunday and not knowing whether anything would be open, the Spanish being very religious and all, we stopped off at a small late-night alimentation for a few slices of synthetic Dutch cheese and a few rolls to make a picnic.

A somewhat confusing football game was on the big screen of the bar we entered. It was definitely Manchester United against Tottenham Hotspur; however, the feed came in from Qatar so the commentary and adverts were incomprehensible. United won 3-1.

The nightcap turned out to be half a bottle of Veterano. This is a brandy from Jerez in the south, the sherry area – Jerez = sherry – it's where the word comes from. In addition, it's not technically a brandy as EU legislation doesn't recognise the 30% alcohol content as sufficient strength and a slur on the name. It's now a 'spirit drink'. We were looking at the bottle when a Spaniard offered his opinion on the subject.

"It is not strong but it is very good." We agreed with him.

We discussed alcohol units and told the Spaniard that the UK government had just reduced the safe level of alcohol consumption to 14 units a week. The Spaniard fell off his stool.

"In Spain, a man is allowed 35 units a week." This did sound more realistic. A quick bit of maths suggested this was about six and a half of these spirit drinks a day, about half the amount in our current glasses.

"Then the wine with the dinner is not included." Hang on. The Spanish government recommend that you can drink up to two and a half times the UK limit plus wine with dinner?

"Sí."

Our friend obviously took advantage of his drinks' allowance and that of some of his friends too.

A Gregorian chant wafted up from the street.

"What the …?" My brandy befuddled brain slowly cranked into gear. I opened the shutters. Six robed monks stood underneath our window signing their blessed hearts out. "It's six o'clock in the bloody morning. On a Sunday." said I somewhat gruffly. It was still dark. And then the bells from the church opposite kicked off. I got up.

We were way too early for breakfast, so we left a note for the proprietor and got off on the road. 23 kilometres today.

An ethereal mist puddled around the narrow streets. Like-minded pilgrims exited their accommodations all awoken at the same ungodly hour by the maddening monks. Zombie-like they shambled along like the crippled and broken living dead of old. None of the Usain Bolt nimbleness of your modern, millennial undead here[1]. Lynne's strained groin allowed her to join in with the lurching, uncoordinated gait.

---

[1] Jamaican sprinter and world record holder. Modern films of the Zombie genre have the undead as super-fast moving beings.

The Queen's Bridge gave the name of the town. This queen, Muniadona, the wife of King Sancho the Great, built a bridge in the eleventh century to aid the poor pilgrims in crossing the Arga river. Whilst such acts were, no doubt, altruistic in nature, having a good bridge, an imposing church and safe town were also good for the coffers and attracted pilgrims to spend time and money in your town rather than at someone else's.

The zombies we had encountered in the town were, in fact, a group of South Koreans, covered from head to toe. Broad brimmed hats, face masks, dark glasses, gloves, not an inch of flesh exposed. Heaven knows from where they got their vitamin D.

The hoped-for café never materialised. Obviously, Spain closed on Sundays. A Citroen Berlingo appeared and the occupant offered vacuum flask coffee and little pre-packaged buns from his open boot. We gave a handful of coins for his thoughtfulness.

The town hall at Cirauqui furnished us with our sellos for the day. This atmospheric hilltop village had been untouched for a thousand years. Stepping back even further in time we crossed a small Roman bridge. Sandals, two millennia old, would have trod this very path. We were walking history.

Whilst the scenery was serene, today was a bit of a slog, mainly as Lynne found it difficult and our pace was slow. We ate our plastic cheese and rock hard rolls with little pleasure on a village bench. Relief came in the shape of an out of the way donativo. The path passed through a pebbled fairy grotto. A bell strung across the path invited us to ring it for '*good vibrations*'. We did and we smiled. Oh, the simple things in life. As we walked off, we heard the fainter and fainter tinkle of it ringing and we smiled again, and again.

As we had set off early, we reached Estella in good time, such good time in fact that a bar was still open for lunch – on a Sunday!

The bar owner welcomed us with a smile, pointed at the beer pumps for approval and started to pour. We refreshed ourselves and refreshed ourselves again. It had been a long walk.

A large gaggle of pilgrims were chatting around wobbly metal tables pushed together and we joined them, space being made for us in an ever increasing circle. Luckily the lingua franca of the Camino was English so we were able to converse with everyone. One group had walked all the way from Roncevalles that day, a 50 kilometre walk, and had still arrived before us.

We gravitated towards a couple of Irish walkers who had met up on the trail, Peter and Colin. Conversation comes easily at the end of a long day, particularly after a beer or two and especially with the Irish. Peter was an occupational therapist and Colin a retired lorry driver. The four of us agreed to meet up that evening for a 'proper drink'. This was never going to end well.

Father Christmas was sitting at the bar as we arrived in good time for our evening rendezvous. It wasn't the actual Father Christmas, but if this chap ever wanted some seasonal work, then he'd get the job straight away. We were chatting to him as Peter and Colin arrived and joined in. We asked where we should eat that evening.

"Try the Horno De San Miguel." he said. "You'll like it."

They weren't exactly run off their feet. We were the only four diners there. If we had been there for a romantic meal, then we would have been disappointed. Any chance of intimacy would have been stifled by the insanely attentive service. A sip of the wine and the glass was refilled, a dish finished and it disappeared before the knife and fork landed. Having said that, there was no pressure on us to hurry up, something some of us would regret later.

There was, as ever, a pilgrims' menu, but this was a notch up from the standard fayre and far better than previously experienced. Large dishes of paella and Asturian bean stew (a smoky sausage and white bean dish) arrived. Not knowing how this worked, we couldn't quite gauge how much to eat. Do we take what we want and then there'll be further dishes or is this it? We worked on the 'this is it' premise. It was a mistake.

The main courses arrived. Rabo de toro (Spanish ox-tail stew) and a casserole made from pork cheek (carrilladas). It dawned on us that we were never going to be able to walk tomorrow, or perhaps the day after. Dessert was crème caramel which, despite us being full to the gunnels, slipped down a treat.

The four of us sat like beached whales unable to do very much other than feel ill. Peter rallied to the cause.

"Nightcaps?"

Pacharán or patxaran (in Basque) came up in conversation at Roncevalles with our Spanish dining companion. This was a traditional Basque digestive made from sloes. At the time we'd not had the opportunity to try it.

"Pacharán?" We asked the proprietor.

"Sí, sí" he replied scuttling off behind the bar to dust off some long forgotten bottle of red liqueur brought back from a unmemorable holiday by a mischievous patron.

'Medicinal' - that was the adjective I was looking for. If I had had a niggling bronchial infection this stuff would have been the cure. I looked at the bottle. 29% it said, even less than the 'spirit drink' from the night before. At this rate we were never going to reach the Spanish Chief Medical Officer's expectations, given that the four bottles of wine with dinner did not count. The proprietor noticed us examining the alcoholic content. 'A challenge' he thought and came over with a bottle of a 40% yellow liqueur. This was the 'los cojones del perro'[1]. We drank the bottle.

Time had flown. It was late, perhaps not for the average Spaniard who was just getting a little peckish, but for pilgrims it was the equivalent of the middle of the night, especially as last night's middle of the night had been ruined by the monk boy band. It was ten thirty.

"Shit." exclaimed Peter and Colin in unison as they looked at their watches and collected their stuff, running out in the direction of their albergue. Our walk back was rather more of a slow drunken tango.

The pacharán was perhaps not the panacea Lynne had hoped for and she decided to give her groin a day of rest. I, however, was looking forward to one of the Camino's highlights.

It's the stuff of dreams, the 'Fuente del Vino'. A hole in the wall that dispenses free red wine to pilgrims and, Camino time being what it is, it was wine o'clock. Well, eight am. There was, in fact, a second spout that had water but, given that you could never be sure of the quality of the water, it was best to drink the wine.

---

[1] The dog's b*****ks. British slang for something being very good.

There was a queue. Why wouldn't there be? I waited patiently for my turn. The wine was… well… drinkable. That's not me being rude, but it wasn't quite Château Lafite Rothschild. Having said that what did I expect from free wine coming out of a hole in a wall? Many filled up a plastic

bottle for later. I was one of the 'many'. Lynne left me at the fountain to catch the bus to our next destination, Los Arcos, and I staggered off drunkenly alone.

Colin staggered in the distance. The pacharán had not had much of a restorative effect on him either, not helped by a top up of free fountain wine. Coffee and cheese rolls helped at a handily placed café en route. I picked up a stamp here and one for Lynne – no one would ever know.

The disparate group from the lunchtime before came and went. Khalid from Saudi Arabia was a Camino pro having walked it countless times. However, Khalid's knees had gone from pro to veteran and were taped from ankle to thigh to allow him to walk the route. He was slow but determined. Perhaps I should have brought a bottle of pacharán with me. He could have rubbed it into his knee.

The path meandered along remote farm tracks with the ubiquitous vineyards and olive groves. Up ahead I saw Peter who was posted as lookout whilst his walking companion of the moment was discretely urinating behind a bush. The three of us settled into a relaxed pace, chatting about life, the universe and everything; well Brexit mainly.

Brierley mentioned a popular mobile café en route and Eduardo, the mobile café owner, was indeed, open for business. Over three freshly squeezed orange juices, Peter filled me in on the antics after he had left us last night.

The municipal albergues have a strict lights out policy. Estella's was ten pm. The pacharán drinking hadn't finished until ten thirty. The door was locked. Malory Towers-like[1] the two Irishmen had to break into the dormitory, no doubt climbing a drainpipe that slowly detached itself from the guttering as they ascended. It looked like detention for them. Again.

Conversations around Brexit were a marvellous time waster. John was very much of the opinion that the UK was mad to want to leave the EU. Peter played honest broker and me, protagonist. The last six kilometres flew by. John told me about the Jewish Italian author, Primo Levi, who survived Auschwitz concentration camp by putting a small stone into his shoe on the basis that he could only concentrate on one pain at a time; the stone hurt more than the treatment he was suffering. John said I was that stone. I didn't know whether to take this as a compliment or insult. John never walked with us again. I'll take it that it was the latter.

At Los Arcos John and Peter rushed off to get as good a bunk as was available at this time of the day and I ambled into town. Lynne was sitting in the square, looking far better for a day off, and had a beer waiting. We ordered a steaming plate of fried potatoes with bacon topped with a cream and blue cheese sauce. It was sunny. All was well with the world.

Our accommodation provider, yes, we'd booked ahead, had suggested a family restaurant for dinner. After putting one foot in front of the other, food was the next most important thing in the life of a pilgrim.

Pilgrims fall into a number of categories. There's the cook it yourself brigade. These can always be found in the convenience store buying: 1) a large bag of pasta, 2) jars of tomato sauce, 3) wine in a plastic container. These pilgrims congregate in the albergue kitchen in the late afternoon and communally add the pasta to water and when cooked and drained stir in the pasta sauce. On occasion, they may add a can of tuna. Don't get me wrong, I am all in favour of the communal eating bit, and I have no issue with the plastic wine. However, eating at five o'clock is just not me, however convivial the conversation.

---

[1] A series of novels by English children's author Enid Blyton about a girls' boarding school.

Next up the pecking order are the pilgrim menuers. These stick to the ten or so euro menu that most restaurants serve. Some meals were very good, others questionable. The menus, on the whole were predictable. I've mentioned the pasta and red sauce. This is a staple as a starter. Others included Russian salad (which I liked) or perhaps a local soup. Next course was usually chicken, quartered (the leg bit) and fried. On occasion this was pork or a bit of dried cod. Finally, a piece of fruit or yoghurt (also often red). The wine was usually out of a box, but on occasion there were some nice surprises.

We were in the next tier, taking advantage of the local cuisine and wine. This was not, on the whole, much pricier than the pilgrim menu and whilst the wine was often more expensive it was no more than you'd pay in the UK and of a much better quality. As an alternative, visiting a more up market establishment and ordering the pilgrim's menu there, would often get great results.

If there was a higher tier then it was unlikely they would encourage the great unwashed. Having said that, we did eat in some very posh establishments and they were very accommodating.

Mavi's wasn't much to look at from the outside, in fact, it wasn't much when we got inside but it did promise something other than macaroni.

"The Spanish don't do vegetables" it is oft said and it's rare to get the equivalent of meat and two veg on a plate. Even vegetarian dishes are often sprinkled with ham or chorizo, so vegetarians have to be careful. Salads do appear regularly but they are never overly exciting. However, Mavi's promised us something green.

The menestra de verduras soup was the sort of dish that a child would have spent hours sitting at the dining table truculently refusing to eat (if, with modern parenting, this happens anymore?). The main ingredient was iron. Just looking at it made you feel fitter. Not only that, it came in a washing up bowl. By the time the veal escalope and arroz con leche were polished off our haemoglobin count must have been off the scale.

Eating in Spain is rarely the intimate, romantic experience one might hope for and, even in quite upmarket restaurants, a television will be flickering in the corner. Most usually, Manchester United were playing someone, but this screen was showing *Ven a Cenar Conmigo*, better known in the UK as *Come Dine with Me[1]*.

Glamour puss and singer Rossana (Roxy) had decided to do something 'experimental'. Rule One: when trying to impress your fellow contestants, stick with something you know. Roxy, of course, fails spectacularly resulting in her leaving the kitchen and buying a dish from a local convenience store. I can't wait to see what happens tomorrow and what score the other contestants give her in the taxi on the way home.

With Mr Creosote-like stomachs we headed for a bar and a Torres ten year old brandy in the vain hope that it would help digest Mavi's gigantean meal. Perhaps two were needed.

The planned 28 kilometres seemed rather ambitious. Perhaps a shorter day was needed as we were still disabled by last night's meal. The plan was to get to Viana and see how we felt.

With an alternative plan in mind, we stayed in the village for coffee and, "oh that custard pastry looks nice". We sat people-watching. Realistically, we didn't need any more food.

Depending on what time of day we started, we saw different types of walker. Early on in the morning we met the keen wiry types either wanting to get on the road to get the best spot at the next albergue or because they had set themselves a Herculean task of walking 30 or 40 kilometres a day. Then there were the late starters who had a leisurely breakfast and then sauntered along the route often being disappointed when accommodation was full at their final destination. My mate Connor (of the book read on the bus) would have fallen into this category. We fell into a middle group that took advantage of the cafés being open for breakfast, lunch and dinner and booked accommodation on-line wherever possible. 'Civilised' is what we called it.

Shirt sleeves were the order of the day with the promise of hotter weather to come. The inclement weather at the start of the walk was a distant memory. With a warm day and fair wind, the Camino was a

---

[1] British reality TV show where amateur chefs host a three-course dinner party for other contestants at their own home.

pleasure to walk. Companions smiled more, birds sung more sweetly and feet hurt less, or at least we didn't notice them hurting so much.

Torres del Rio greeted us with a cluster of sand-coloured buildings set in an emerald green plain. Whilst our forebears may not have stopped for a cortado, they would have certainly rested here and looked out onto the same vista. But it was the Templar church, the Iglesia de Santo Sepulcro, that they would have remembered. Built in the twelfth century, it looked remarkably modern to my eyes and must have been positively futuristic to a medieval pilgrim. Octagonal in design it struck me as being more Moorish than Christian and I half expected to hear a call to prayer from the local muadhdhin.

Refreshed both physically and spiritually, we continued onwards, light of step knowing that we would be in Viana by lunchtime and could have a relaxing rest of the day. These last ten kilometres took us through gently rolling countryside, mainly arable fields of early wheat and still dormant vineyards; the plants, like us, waiting for spring to arrive properly. But signs of winter were still visible on the mountain tops in the distance.

A well maintained chapel (Nuestra Senora del Poyo) sat at the side of the road, a stone bench and table bathed in the warm late morning sun. Delving into our rucksacks we retrieved bread and cheese and the bottle of free fountain wine. If you could encapsulate what the Camino was about this would be it. Two modern hobos, with their worlds on their backs, stopping for the simplest of meals and not a care in the world – *We'd like to be unhappy but we never do have the time[1]*. Umm, another ear worm.

Something was amiss. We crossed into a steep ravine and zig-zagged down to the bottom. However, instead of skipping down in my usual carefree manner, I felt a blister on my little toe. Just the start of one. I was loath to mention it as Lynne had been complaining about her groin, boots and blisters since Day Two. I did mention it. It was a mistake.

Viana thronged with meandering pilgrims. We now had a choice; did we continue and walk the ten kilometres to Logroño or did we sit

---

[1] Busy Doing Nothing", a song by Bing Crosby from the 1949 film, *A Connecticut Yankee in King Arthur's Court.*

in the warm sun, with an ice cold beer and chill out for the rest of the day?

Slog versus beer?

We booked into the Palacio de Pujadas. For a few seconds we thought about all those authentic pilgrims plodding their way on to Logroño and fighting for the best bunk in an overcrowded, smelly, noisy dormitory. Not that this hotel was perfect. It lacked 'personality'. 'Corporate' was how I described it. It did, however, have air conditioning, fluffy towels and posh little toiletries. We would live with the guilt.

With clean and sanitary surroundings, my first priority was to sort out the very small blister on my little toe. Speak to any pilgrim for more than fifteen seconds and the conversation will gravitate to blisters. Search for 'blisters' and 'Camino' on Google and half a million hits are found. Whatever you do though; DO NOT click on 'images'!

Evidently, there are three types of blister; roof intact, roof torn and deroofed. Every pilgrim should have a 'blister plan' and depending on the type of blister, different approaches are needed. My blister was a little one and of the 'roof intact' variety. Therefore, all it needed was draining (Savlon and a needle) and then plastering up. Some sites suggested threading cotton to the needle and then leaving the thread in place, through the skin to aid draining. Nasty.

The pilgrim's plaster of choice is Compeed. This is a sort of second skin using, wait for it, hydrocolloid technology. Basically, it is really sticky stuff that won't come off after a day's sweaty walking.

With my foot now mended and a refreshing shower I decided to continue with my Hemingway book, depressing though the characters had become. Lady Brett Ashley, twice divorced, was looking for a new husband; one who will keep her in the style to which she had become accustomed. Said husband will not be too demanding and let her have extra marital relations with whomsoever she likes. At the moment she's having a dalliance with a young bullfighter, Romero.

With the sun dipping behind the tall buildings, the narrow streets had cooled and were now silent, the majority of pilgrims a good ten kilometres away. Brierley informed us that the town's most famous resident was Cesare Borgia, part of the famous Italian religious family. Cesare became a cardinal on his father's (Rodrigo) elevation to the Papacy. My knowledge of this family came from the 1980's BBC television series *The Borgias* which, if I remember rightly, mainly consisted of sixteenth century rumpy pumpy, Machiavellian plots and murdering anyone who got in their way.

The town was carved out of rock and after an aperitif beer served by an incomprehensible Chinese gentleman in a local bar, we entered the subterranean vaults of the Casa Armendariz with its baronial comedor (dining room) and domed ceilings, lit by sconces on the bare stone walls. The pilgrim menu was handwritten and twelve euros. There were vegetables. We jumped at the chance of again having something green.

We were surrounded by the normal array of nationalities, five Brits, a group of three Germans and a couple from San Francisco who spent the entire meal talking about 'business technologies' and 'digital frontlines' in decibels far too loud for the location or the occasion. Many come to the Camino to escape the outside world. These hadn't. I was tempted to go over to them and tell them they were being idiots. I had a brandy instead.

By the time we arose most of the pilgrims in Logroño would have packed up their sweaty sleeping bags, squeezed their tired feet into even more tired boots and been on the road for an hour or so - full of pious self righteousness. We lounged around and had warm, soft croissants, freshly squeezed orange juice and just ground, dark roast coffee. I scanned El Pais for an update on the news. I understood little of it. For 'little' read 'none'.

My blister had healed nicely. I told Lynne. I'm not sure she was listening.

From the ruins of San Pedro we had a 360 degree view. The town behind us, honey coloured stone, radiant with the early morning sun and to the south west, a vast plain with Logroño in the near invisible distance.

A languid form walked ahead of us. We knew the gait.

"Colin." I hailed.

Colin told us that he had had his luggage transferred to Navarrete (20 kilometres away) and was much happier now that he had got the weight off his back. We were later to find out that he had a lot of weight to get off his chest as well.

The plain's green we had seen from our elevated starting point were vineyards and at this time of the year they were just starting to bud.

"We are walking at the same speed as things grow," observed Lynne, very sagely. We'd started out in snow in the east and as we moved further west and into the sun, plants had started to spring into life. The three of us, in shirt sleeves, were in no hurry and were at peace with the world.

A group of Koreans passed us. Well, we presumed they were Korean, with their wide brimmed hats, bandanas, dark sun glasses and black gloves. These were not at one with nature. They had done everything they could to keep nature out. It felt kind of sad.

A donativo on the path leading down into Logroño gave us our stamp for the day. It also gave us an additional rest as Colin left his credential there and had to return to pick it up. Our passports were already becoming valuable and there was probably a burgeoning black market in part-completed credentials.

In stark relief against the cloudless pale blue sky were the unkempt nests of families of storks, precariously built atop electricity pylons. The birds preened themselves as we passed by and occasionally launched off to fly around in a tight circle to gracefully land back in their nest.

A pilgrim information office stood at the bridge into the village and Colin decided to check on bus times to his overnight stop as he was going further than us. We mooched whilst he was inside. Our day was then our own and we could relax. Colin decided to relax with us. We soon learned what Irish relaxation consisted of. But first the cathedral.

From the bright sunlight of outside, the interior of the Santa María de la Redonda was dark and gloomy. This we found was a cunning ploy by the administrators of the building who charged a euro to light the interior on a time switch. Very entrepreneurial. Other than that, it was a church: vaulted ceilings, lots of seats, little rooms and pictures. Perhaps I was getting a little churched out.

Opposite the church was a large square and so we made for a group of tables and a beer. Well, it was two minutes to eleven.

"Two large beers and a small one please." said I in my best Spanish.

"No." said the waiter. We were about to get shirty. "No. It is happy hour. It is half price for pints". We loved the way that the Spanish always referred to large beers as pints or pintas.

We ordered three of them. By five past eleven Colin had finished his and ordered three more. I could see how relaxed we were going to get. However, on the basis that you drink at the speed of the fastest drinker, I had soon caught up. Lynne was stacking them up.

With the relaxation came conversation. Many people walking the Camino had a back story. In fact, Lynne and I were two of the few that did not. We were just going on a very long walk.

Colin's son had been murdered two years previously and this was the second anniversary of his death. Colin had decided that he could not bear to be in Ireland to remember this awful event and had booked an open ticket to Spain and would walk until he felt it was time to go back home. There was little we could say after this so we drank our beer and a subsequent beer in companionable silence.

After we had relaxed sufficiently, we then drank the beers that Lynne had amassed. Colin went off to catch his bus.

Heads needed to be cleared, so we lurched around the city getting our bearings. Our bearings got, we needed something to soak up the alcohol. Tapas.

We were in the capital of Rioja, and when in Rioja we felt it would be churlish not to try a glass. Lynne had white, I had a red. We toasted an absent friend (Steve), a friend who had loved Rioja, a friend who was being cremated that very day back in England. He would have been very happy we were raising a glass to him, and very cheesed off that he wasn't with us.

The goats' cheese, artichoke and bacon on toast was not quite soaking up the alcohol, so more tapas were needed. Unfortunately, more tapas came with more wine. Steve would have been proud of us. The next instalment was a plate of deep fried pork scratchings, black pudding, tortilla on toast and lightly battered cod. If this didn't soak up the alcohol, nothing would. It didn't. Nothing would.

I woke up in some child's bedroom. Tintin posters covered the walls. Perhaps I was still asleep and this was a dream. No, the private room in the albergue was decorated for a ten year old.

I thought perhaps I needed a little more beer as the wine at lunchtime was quite dehydrating. So, after a refreshing shower we headed back into town.

It was still happy hour.

Time for some proper bar hopping along the Calle Laurel.

We'd been to Logroño before - on our aborted China trip. We'd loved it then and searched out some of the places that we vaguely remembered. Whereas, many places in Spain give free tapas when ordering a drink, here in the bigger cities, the tapas is the reason for the visit and you pay for the food.

Themed bars were the name of the game. Each establishment specialised in a particular type of tapas. One specialised in potatoes, another octopus and then there was the Bar Angel. This bar's speciality was mushrooms. A utilitarian looking place but lively with most punters eating the same dish, a slice of French stick with a kebab skewer of mushrooms and prawns covered in garlic butter. We ordered the same and were soon wiping messy fingers with hopelessly inefficient little napkins.

Neither of us mentioned it, but we were both in search of one particular bar. "It's the pig nose bar." cried Lynne as she recognised the unassuming institution of our skewed memory. This was the bar of legend, the bar that served the equivalent of the Roman delicacies in Monty Python's *Life of Brian*: "*… otters' noses, jaguars' earlobes, wolf nipple chips - get them while they're hot*". Bar Sebas sells the sort of meat product that usually comes under the definition of 'rendered' as part of some industrialised process to make glue. They also do a mean tortilla, and these were flying out of the takeaway serving hatch as quickly as they could make them. I needed tortilla. I also fancied some of the more esoteric meat dishes. This was not a stop for the faint hearted.

A plate of lambs' ears with green peppers appeared before me. 'Cartilage with a hint of ovine cerumen (sheep's earwax), fried in a light batter', I wrote in my diary. This place was a Labrador retriever's dream. The peppers were nice. We tried pigs' snouts, bits of stomachs, blood sausage and, of course the famous Tortilla de Patatas.

They call the tapas route here 'La Senda de los Elefantes' - the Trail of the Elephants - pachyderm-like diners staggering from one bar to the next picking bits of discarded knee replacement surgery from their teeth.

More than ever, we needed a brandy and a coffee to rid us of the taste, and memory, of the ears. Or, perhaps… some cheese. La Casa de los Quesos was just around the corner and were offering a 'degustacion de quesos' (cheese tasting).

"Welcome, welcome." Agustín, the proprietor, swept us in. "Wine?" He was speaking our language, well, something approaching English at least. Two glasses of something red appeared from his nano-bar followed by a platter of goats' and sheep's cheese from Galica and Catalonia. "Yes", they sometimes had West Country Cheddar and  Somerset brie Agustín explained – we were now speaking fluent cheese.

In a mixture of bad English and non-existent Spanish, Agustín and I discussed the relative merits of various Chris Rea songs of which we both knew two. The same two. This was a two minute conversation at best. An hour later and after a couple more wines we decided our favourite was *On the Beach* – or it might have been *Road to Hell*.

LOGROÑO – BURGOS

Belgian cartoon characters being chased by earless sheep induced by too much cheese would have passed into post dream forgetfulness had I not scribbled down the recollection in my diary as soon as I awoke.

Whilst we had to be flexible, there was a definite plan for the journey. I had even created an Excel spreadsheet. This identified the ideal mileage per day, weekly key destinations and rest days. The journey, like this book, was split between the seven large town/cities along the route. In between, each section contained a rest day (expected to be in the large conurbations) and a 'padding' day, an extra day with nothing planned. Either this could be an additional rest day or allowed us two easy days, or three not so strenuous days. It was an ergonomic work of art.

The two days before Logroño had used one of the padding days and the plan was to spend two days in the city here. However, we'd done the major sights and were offalled out. Another night of Tintin didn't appeal and we decided to head out for the open road and the peace of the Camino. We were also keen to get on with walking as being stuck in one place was beginning to feel alien to us. We were becoming true nomads.

Roaming on my phone had gone on the blink. Not that this was a major issue, but there was no Wi-Fi and we needed to find some accommodation for the night. Heaven knows what your average Medieval pilgrim did without 4G. It was too early to call the provider's help-line. We would have to do this en route.

We'd liked Logroño. It was a pleasant, unassuming city and as we exited though the suburbs, we joined a host of late middle aged walkers, cyclists and joggers all undertaking gentle exercise in a country park. Perhaps that's why we hadn't seen many overweight and obese people on our journey. Perhaps it was because the pigs' ears were inedible and thus calorie free.

"…And it's a beautiful day here in Spain." I was speaking to an adviser at my mobile provider in the UK, who was sorting out why roaming wasn't working.

"It is here too." he responded. Damn, there is little point in gloating about the weather if the recipient is experiencing the same good fortune. However, I bet his little cubicle in Swindon was not as pleasant as the café by the Pantano de la Grajera, the reservoir used to water the nearby orchards. Roaming fixed, we were on our way again.

Chain link fences along the route were nearly always repurposed as makeshift pilgrim shrines and passers-by would weave sticks collected from the route into crosses. Brierley commented in his guide that the crosses are a '*symbol of the greater mystery that lies beyond the business and suffering of this world*'. I thought that probably someone had made one once and others had just copied them.

The Spanish skyline would not be the same without the huge cut out black bulls (with their equally large testicles) gracing hillsides and we passed one such silhouetted against the cloudless baby blue sky as we entered the outskirts of Navarrete. These advertising hoardings started to appear in Spain in 1956 and were used to promote the Veterano brandy/spirit liqueur that we were very much becoming accustomed to. They nearly had their day in 1994 when the Spanish government banned the roadside advertising of alcoholic drinks. However, after a legal battle, a Spanish court allowed them to stay as part of the cultural heritage of the country.

In the outskirts of the town, we came across the ruins of a medieval monastery and hospital, the Order of San Juan de Acre. This was founded in 1185 for the treatment of pilgrims walking the Camino. Lynne would have been happy if they could have sorted out her aches and pains. However, the next building was the Bodega of Don Jacob, the local wine producer, the products of which were the next best thing.

Peace reigned in Navarrete's central square. A few pilgrims meandered about and it was getting to lunchtime. However, first things first; a trip to the pharmacy. Lynne had got to the point of needing some professional advice about her groin rather than my home-spun remedies and heavy reliance on wine and beer as being the panacea for everything.

Crippled pilgrims were the pharmacist's bread and butter.

"Too heavy", the white coated pharmacist told Lynne as he expertly weighed her rucksack, grunting theatrically and wiping his brow. "It should be no more than ten percent of your body weight." As if he knew how much she weighed.

This ten percent rule appears all over the internet, forums and countless books about the Camino. In theory it makes sense to limit the amount of weight on your back, but it all seemed a bit arbitrary to me. We saw some walkers with packs the size of pencil cases (although they were probably having their luggage transferred) and others with pantechnicon sized rucksacks containing the kitchen sink.

In reality, it is impossible to only carry ten percent of your body weight when walking for a couple of months. I am 73 kilos and therefore my rucksack should have been no more than about seven and a half kilos. I carried one change of clothes (solar-dry, polyester) and a few extra pairs of lightweight underpants and wicking tee shirts and a pair of sandals. I had an ultra-light sleeping bag, microfibre towel, a few toiletries, my tablet-cum-phone-cum-Kindle (and charger) a plastic mug and spork (spoon/fork/knife in one), the guide book and my diary. These weighed just under nine kilos. It would have been impossible for me to take any less.

Some take this weight thing to extremes. The Brierley comes with a 'cut-out' introduction (little scissor marks along the spine) and some people tear out pages after they have read them along the way – probably using them as toilet paper. Others cut the handles off their toothbrushes, remove any spare straps from rucksacks and even take staples out of any papers they are carrying. To be fair, Lynne's rucksack was heavier than mine due to the stuff girls have to take: hairdryer, travel iron, straighteners/curlers, hair care products, ball gown in case we went somewhere posh...

The pharmacist recommended a knee brace from the Rafael Nadal[1] range of super expensive Bionic Man[2] aids and gave her some ibuprofen pills the size of horse tablets. These, of course, added additional weight to her bag. So, with our purchases and sage advice we went off to the Bar Deportivo to drink and forget the huge amount we'd just spent enriching Rafael Nadal.

Our hostel for the night was brand new, it had been only open for a few days and was run by a young and very chatty Englishman. We telephoned from the bar to see if they had rooms. He had.

"Fancy a beer?" I said to him on the spur of the moment.

"Yes." He said, I'll see you in a couple of minutes. So, we sat, the dark shadows of our table umbrella contrasting with the pale paving slabs at our feet. It was a beautiful day.

The Posada Ignatius Guesthouse was a bit of a find. It was originally a palace owned by the Duke of Nájera during the 15th Century. Many of the original features were still intact and Danny (our host) proudly took us on a guided tour of the house and the extensive wine cellars. This was the best place we'd stayed at and it was very unlikely we would stay anywhere better during our walk.

Well rested, we took an early evening stroll around the medieval heritage of the town that had been well preserved, nestled in amongst the vineyards, with the church at its centre. However, it didn't take long to explore and we soon found ourselves back at the Bar Deportivo, its pollarded plane trees just showing the first signs of spring. In a few months their lush green shoots would have grown along the wires strung across the square and created a natural leaf canopy to protect drinkers from the harsh Spanish sun.

The bar specialised in paella and so we had two raciones together with a bottle of the Don Jacob from the winery we had passed on the way in. Danny joined us again after dinner with his one year old and we passed the rest of the evening chatting with locals and pilgrims, now all friends.

Lynne decided that perhaps her bag was too heavy to carry and contacted a luggage transfer service. These companies advertise in

---

[1] Spanish professional tennis player.
[2] From the 1970's TV series *The Six Million Dollar Man*.

most of the accommodation providers and all work on a similar principle; you bung a five euro note into an envelope with the next destination identified, tie it to your rucksack and leave the bag in reception in the morning. Lynne chose Jacotrans and they said they would love to provide a service. I continued with the full Camino experience, carrying my rucksack, however overweight it was.

There is something liberating about putting on a rucksack and carrying all your worldly belongings with you. Just slipping the straps over your shoulders promotes a feeling of independence and adventure and puts a spring into your step. Yes, there are occasions when it's a bit of a trudge, but the sense of achievement when the bag is taken off at a destination is worth it. Lynne was going to miss all that.

Being British, the provision of a proper breakfast was part of Danny's DNA. The table was laden with: cold meats, eggs, cheese, speciality breads and very good coffee. We'd had such a good time that we felt a bit awful letting him know that there was no hot water and the toilet seat had fallen off. We put it down to snagging.

As we left, we asked for a stamp for our passport.

"Sorry," said Danny, "… we've ordered it and it hasn't arrived yet." Disappointing, but not the end of the world, we'd get our stamp later in the day. As we were about to leave, the postman arrived and delving into his sack pulled out a parcel with the self-inking stamp. With great pride Danny stamped both our credentials. Kismet – that's what it was.

We had 15 flat kilometres to cover today. Our companions were Tempranillo, Garnacha, Mazuelo and Graciano vine varieties, all part of the classic Rioja wine makeup. At approximately four kilometres an hour we would be at our destination by lunchtime easily. But it was far too nice a day to rush and we adopted a leisurely ambling pace, absorbing the tranquillity of the route, nodding at passing pilgrims and just being content. It was a lovely state to be in. Lynne was positively bouncing with lightness.

We were also supposed to be following the highly promoted *Ruta del Arte* but for the life of us we couldn't spot any. Lynne suggested that perhaps they had run out of money after putting up all the signs.

The Bodegas Alvia was an innocent distraction with its plywood cut-out of a Medieval pilgrim drinking from an elevated wine skin. We poked our heads through and had our photos taken, every single one an advertisement for the winery. Unfortunately, the shop was closed so we were unable to buy a bottle for a picnic, and at any rate, Lynne now didn't have room in her miniature day sack for a bottle. Her loss.

The Camino attracts journalists and film-makers in their droves. Not only does the route have magnificent scenery but also great scope for shots of very tired looking people, all of whom have a back story.

When we were learning Spanish for the trip, we spent time watching RTVE's[1] *Buen Camino* with Marta Márquez. This had all the requisite characters: a father and son team, a pilgrim with one leg and plenty of tears and people saying they couldn't continue. Whilst I said that I watched it to improve my Spanish, most male viewers were probably more interested in Marta's shorts which were the shortest I'd ever seen.

At Nájera we were drinking a beer at a pavement café. Two individuals laden with cameras and microphones flopped in the seats next to us. They had obviously had a hard day; not only had they walked the Camino, they had also lugged tons of equipment with them as well.

Camino Skies was the film; a New Zealand/Australian production following six participants walking all 800 kilometres of the route. Each had a particular reason for walking: Claude (voyage of discovery), Julie (loss of husband), Terry (loss of granddaughter), Mark (loss of stepdaughter), Cheryl (had climbed three of the highest

---

[1] Spanish Radio and Television Corporation.

mountains in the world) and Susan (severe degenerative arthritis). None of them were just out for a good walk like us.

Nájera, originally Naxara, meaning 'town between the rocks', had been hewn from the surrounding hillside, the red stone of the buildings replicating that of the sandstone surrounding the town. The place felt a little hemmed in and claustrophobic. Perhaps, because of this, the place had a strategic military position and the Romans, Saracens and, of course, Roland (Charlemagne's mate), had been there long before us.

Accommodation for that night was in the somewhat euphemistically named 'nightclub district'. Whether this would prove to be an opportunity to let our hair down and see a bit of nightlife or stop us from getting much needed sleep, only time would tell.

As I lay on my bed killing time between doing nothing that afternoon and nothing in the evening, I scrolled though the photos taken thus far, deleting those that needed deleting, making backups and cataloguing. I came across the pictures of the Koreans walking in the mist back at Punte la Reina. I scribbled down *'The Camino de Zombiago'*[1]. It'd make a great book title.

The echoing town square buzzed with the hundreds of pilgrims and locals all soaking up the last rays of the sun. Tables sprawled haphazardly, not necessarily geographically adjacent to the bar owning them. A waiter turned up.

"What beers do you have?"

"Normal."

"We'll have two normal beers then please." I was not sure that he was really cut out to be a waiter.

Chatting to a couple of pilgrims earlier in the day, they had recommended the Mesón El Buen Yantar for dinner and we headed off to investigate.

Bonus number one – we got a one euro discount for producing our credential at the Yantar. Bonus number two – it was good food. I had the San Jacobos (breaded loin of pork stuffed with cheese and ham). I

---

[1] © Ian Pearson 2022.

avoided the *Stuffed Peppers with Meth* from the menu. Perhaps later after a bit of dancing we'd need something to keep us going.

We were raring to go. It was Friday night, we were well fed and rested, and we were in the nightclub district. It was closed. In fact, the whole town was closed. We walked around a bit looking for a bar for a nightcap and coffee. Nothing. Nada. Perhaps we were too early? Yes, that must have been it.

A full Brierley section today of 21 kilometres, hence up and ready for the off by seven. We had not been woken up in the early hours by hoards of drunken party goers. Perhaps Saturday night was the big one and we'd arrived a day too soon?

The streets were eerily quiet. Very similar to ten o'clock the night before. The town was bathed in a roseate glow both from the rising sun and the surrounding hills. No open café was to be had, so we left sleepy Nájera behind.

It was a couple of hours before we came across a café and could soak up the first caffeine of the day. Along with the lack of green vegetables we could also have done with a bit of fibre. At home breakfast would be porridge or shredded wheat. Here, our first meal of the day was more often than not a sugary, white processed bread bun. I was a little concerned that I might develop type 2 diabetes by the end of the journey, although that didn't stop me from devouring the delicious pain au chocolat in front of me. The energy hit was instantaneous, and dangerous. I could do anything. I was Sugarman.

Being brought up in Kent, I recognised the next vista. Tall wooden poles, perhaps three, four metres high, wires holding them together sat in a field by the road. Hops. I had hoped to see a lot of these as we progressed along the path, but these were the first, although just green spears in the dusty soil at the moment. Perhaps I could get my hands on a couple of hundred grams of the dried product. That would be a memento.

We were back in the town that had sparked off my interest in the Camino eight years previously, Santo Domingo de la Calzada – the home of the chickens. We were earlier than expected and had a light lunch of cute quails' eggs and chorizo on slices of fresh French bread. That hit the spot.

A vending machine opposite the café caught my attention. This was obviously stocked for the modern day, out of hours pilgrim: soft drinks, crisps, nuts, chocolate, sandwiches and pasta meals obviously catered for those who were hungry. Compeed plasters and other medical supplies would patch up those who were ailing and then there were essential items for the lonely pilgrim: condoms, vibrators, furry handcuffs, jiggle balls[1] and blow up dolls. Just in case you'd forgotten to pack them. None of these, I hasten to add, were listed in Brierley's checklist of Camino essentials.

A blast furnace greeted us in our apartment for the night. This was pumping out industrial volumes of heat and had no thermostat. We managed to turn it off, opened all the windows and after half an hour or so were able to re enter the room without fainting.

The apartment also had a washing machine and after nearly two weeks of hand washing this was too great an opportunity to miss. We tipped out our bags and put everything we owned into the machine, popped in a liquid detergent capsule (we'd brought four of these from home) and closed the door. We should have known things were not quite right when the fifteen minute quick wash took an hour and a half and then the spin cycle didn't work. We were therefore left with a pile of soggy clothes, all our clothes. By this time the blast furnace heater had lost all its heat and we were unable to relight it. This was not good. It was also getting a bit chilly.

We hung out the clothes knowing they were still going to be wet the following day and went in search of provisions for the following day, a Sunday. A packet of fried egg flavour crisps took my fancy. Reading the ingredients, the pack informed me that the contents may contain traces of egg. Egg of all things in a packet of fried egg crisps!

Before dinner we needed to visit the town's most famous attraction; the cathedral and the chickens. Legend had it that in the fourteenth century a German pilgrim was passing through the town with his parents. Whilst staying at a hostal, a rather amorous Spanish lass

---

[1] Look it up.

propositioned the German boy who politely rebuffed her advances. Being a bit cheesed off at this, the girl planted a silver cup in the boy's sack and then accused him of stealing it. The boy was tried and sentenced to death by hanging.

At some stage the parents noticed their son had not followed them and returned to the town to find their son hanging on the gallows but still alive thanks to Saint Domingo who had patently held the boy up. They rushed to the local magistrate to tell him of the miracle. The magistrate refused to believe the parents and said that "Your son was no more alive than this rooster and chicken that I was just about to eat." With that, the cooked birds jumped up and started crowing. And everyone lived happily ever after. Since that date the church has kept a live cock and hen at the rear of the building. Perhaps cock and bull[1] would be a better combination.

Water dripped off the clothes as I pegged them to my rucksack. Lynne had stuffed her wet clothes into her bag to be transferred to the next stop, the hamlet of Quintanilla del Monte. My stuff would be dry by the end of the day.

It's a Wonderful World by Louis Armstrong filled the air as we reached the linear village of Grañón, the outdoor speakers of the My Way Bar pumping out jazz standards, pilgrims of all nationalities seated outside, chatting and soaking up the sun. If you had to encapsulate what walking the Camino was all about, it would have been that moment. And the coffee was very good too.

I could have sat there all day, but we had ten kilometres ahead of us and Sundays were always a bit hit and miss when it came to provisions. However, we needn't have worried as a few yards up the road we came across the Panaderia Jesús selling delicious freshly baked loaves. All we needed now were some fishes and we could have fed the whole Camino!

Today we were to cross out of Rioja and into Castilla y León, the next department and largest autonomous region in Spain. A large

---

[1] A fanciful story. Origin: two coaching inns (the Cock and the Bull) in Stony Stratford, Buckinghamshire, England had a reputation for travellers telling more and more exaggerated and fanciful stories.

white orientation board marked our progress from one to another and we would spend the next few weeks in this part of Spain. I hoped the wine would be as good.

The Camino has had a heightened exposure over the past few years in the UK. Emilio Estevez filmed *The Way*, the story of four modern day pilgrims walking the route – a sort of re-imagining of the *Wizard of Oz*[1] with each character looking for some sort of meaning in their lives.

The story follows Martin Sheen's[2] character, an American ophthalmologist, as he travels to France to pick up his son's ashes after a fatal accident on the Camino. Sheen fails to understand his son's wanderlust, but on the spur of moment decides to complete the route in homage to his son, depositing little piles of his ashes along the way.

The three companions, met by Sheen en route, encapsulate the essence of the kind of life changing hopes that many pilgrims have: The Canadian woman wants to give up smoking but makes no effort to do so. Likewise, the Dutchman needs to lose weight but loves food too much and the extremely annoying Irishman with writer's block abandons his novel idea to write a book about his experiences along the Way.

It is this last character that is most upon our minds today as our lunch stop was a huge cathedral-like edifice of hay bales in the middle of nowhere. It was here that the writer meets the rest of the characters whilst trying to get inspiration for the next line of his book.

A kindly Dutchman offered to take our photo.

"This will be one of the defining photographs of

---

[1] 1939 American musical fantasy film.
[2] American actor and also the father of Emilio Estevez who directed, produced and wrote *The Way*.

your trip." He said to us. He was, of course, correct.

We ate our cheese and Jesus' bread as others passed by, all seeming to have seen the film and commenting. We took photos for each other, not because of the film, per se, but because it was such an iconic sight. Alright, it was because of the film.

While the Camino often has a quaint naivety to it, and, when I say 'quaint' I also mean downright annoying on occasion, every so often some event wanted you to say "Good on you". The enterprising albergue owner driving up and down the path handing out free bottles of water with the name of his accommodation on the label was one. Had we not have booked that night's bed, we would probably have stayed there.

Science tells us the thing that makes a cold beer refreshing is the carbonic acid created in the mouth from the release of the carbon dioxide bubbles. However, the location, events and companions are also spiritually refreshing and, as we sat outside the bar, large San Miguels in hand, the sun playing on our faces and the six Irish women laughing and joking with us, I thought that, probably, nothing could refresh our parts[1] more than this.

We'd over-walked the path by a kilometre to find the bar for lunch and now retraced our steps to find the hamlet of Quintanilla del Monte and our bed and breakfast, La Aldea Encantada. The near forgotten single track road was our route to the equally near forgotten village. Time had ravaged its amenities; an Italianate church, once the epicentre of all village life, was slowly folding in on itself, a thin band of plastic 'keep out' tape ineffectually trying to keep it upright. This was rural Spain dying before our very eyes.

Anna met us at the door. Tonight, we would live with her family and we had prepared for just this situation. Unfortunately, we hadn't prepared enough.

Six months prior to starting our trip I had picked up the phone.

"I understand you give Spanish lessons."

"Sí."

---

[1] A reference to a UK beer advertising campaign: *Heineken Refreshes the Parts Other Beers Cannot Reach.*

Lander was Basque. Lander was not a man to concern himself with verbs and grammar. Lander was an immersive teacher. From the first minute of arriving at our house, we were speaking Spanish – well he was speaking Spanish and we were bewildered.

"¿Puedo tomar una taza de café por favor?" We got the gist and made him a cup of coffee. "See," he said "...you can understand Spanish."

Lander visited pubs with us (in rural Somerset) and got us to order beers in Spanish from bemused bar staff, took us to supermarkets to point out and name vegetables and demanded a postcard from anywhere we visited: describing the weather, how we got there and what we'd done. He even invited himself and his girlfriend to dinner and stayed the night to show how much the Basques could drink. Note to self; they can drink quite a bit.

Within six months we'd picked up a rudimentary grasp of the language. The sort of grasp that perhaps a Spaniard learning English from a Glaswegian welder would have trying to converse with a Devonshire farmer[1].

A rumble of thunder boomed through the valley.

"¿Lloverá hoy?" [will it rain today?] says I.

"No va a llover." [No, it will not rain] says Anna.

It poured down. Perhaps she didn't understand the question. Perhaps she didn't speak Lander. Perhaps she was just not very good at weather forecasting.

Damp weather was not going to do Lynne any favours as she pulled out her still wet clothing from her rucksack and draped it around the room. I folded up my bone dry kit. I didn't say a word.

Anna fussed around us and herded us into chairs around an antique table. There was no menu. Lumps of very Spanish, very hard cheese arrived together with a bottle of rustic red. A very rich ratatouille with a fried egg on top came next. Then meatballs in a deep red tomato sauce and a single slice of carrot (part of my five a day). Finally, a plain yoghurt. This was probably the most authentic meal of the walk

---

[1] Glasgow in Scotland and Devon in the south west of England.

so far, eating in the owner's dining room, surrounded by her nick-nacks and family photos.

We negotiated about breakfast time. We wanted seven thirty. Anna did breakfast at eight thirty. We compromised and agreed on breakfast at eight thirty.

The Hemingway needed finishing and with absolutely nothing else to do we lay in bed listening to the rain which was not forecast. This had been a good day. We were happy.

Scrambled eggs this morning for breakfast. There was no hurrying; perhaps we needed to chill a bit. It took a good ten minutes of gushing thanks, hand shaking, hugs and the taking of photos with Anna before we could get on our way.

'Flat and boring' is how some pilgrims described these middle stages. However, the boring bit is just a state of mind and the flat bit is a real bonus when you need to crunch the miles (kilometres). 'Yes' there was quite a bit of road walking to come and 'yes' juggernauts did have a habit of screaming past but the lorries were sporadic and all the traffic was doing was following an ancient path. No doubt medieval pilgrims complained about the number of carts on the route.

'Flat and open' is probably what the pilgrims of old hankered after. Dense forests, mountain passes and hidden gullies were ideal for hiding bandits who preyed on the lone walker. Most pilgrims travelled in groups or hired bodyguards. And, it wasn't just the rich who had to worry. Your average bandit would think nothing of killing you for a pair of worn out sandals.

A cat and dog took a fancy to me at Belorado as we stopped for a coffee. I fed them the free piece of cake that came with my cortado.

Perhaps it was the food rather than my caring personality that had attracted them? The village had celebrated the passing of thousands of pilgrims by casting their feet and shoes in bronze along the pavement.

Another casa rural awaited us that night. Perhaps not as friendly as Anna's, in fact we didn't see a soul, but welcoming all the same. I had a shower. I had a rash on my arm. On closer inspection it was a series of minuscule bites. Bed bugs!

After blisters the next most feared affliction, and topic of many a conversation, was that of bed bugs. These are relatively harmless creatures, but can cause an allergic reaction in some people and the bites can be a bit itchy.

Permethrin is the nuclear option when it comes to these little critters. It's a military strength insecticide which kills insects on contact. Lynne and I had doused everything we owned in this before leaving home: clothes, sleeping bags and the rucksacks themselves. We'd also taken all the normal precautions: checking beds and mattresses, not putting rucksacks on the bed and generally staying away from some of the dodgier albergues. However, bed bugs are no respecters of class and a five-star hotel is as likely to have them as the cheapest dormitory. I had no idea where my bites came from. I wasn't going to die from them.

The lorries rumbled past as we sat outside the bar by our accommodation, our faces turned to the last dying rays of the sun. However, we were a little worried about getting carbon monoxide poisoning so we retreated indoors to finish our beers and to see what was for dinner.

Like many traditional restaurants in Spain, many bars had a white tableclothed comedor attached to them and when we asked about food we were shown into the dining room. These establishments always looked as if they hadn't changed much since the 1950s, nor had the menus. I had potatoes and cauliflower which came boiled, and a very nice lamb shank followed by a personal favourite, arroz con leche – rice pudding.

Over our nightcap the proprietor warned me that the area was going to be subject to thunderstorms the following day. However, with the poor level of forecasting that most Spanish exhibited, I was not overly worried.

We were on a mission. We had some ancestors to meet and some skeletons in the closet to confront. But first wolves.

The mist was otherworldly as we passed through the forest of sessile oaks. It would burn off in the morning sun, but now dampened everything, including all sound; so much different from last night's incessant rumble of tyres. We stopped at the Fuente de Mojapan (the moisten bread fountain) where, in former times, you would have waited for other pilgrims to travel with you in order to fend off the hungry wolves. Yes, life was definitely harder back in the day. All we had to worry about now was a blister or two from our Gore-Tex boots and perhaps the bite of a harmless bug that had not succumbed to industrial grade DDT.

At the highest point we reached the Monumento a los Caídos, a monument to those who had fallen in the Spanish Civil War in 1936. This stark edifice was both a reminder of the carnage that occurred in Spain eighty years ago and also acted as a gravestone for those who were summarily executed at that spot.

Despite the gloomy history of the place, the view was lovely and we sat and ate our custard pastries in the peace and quiet, with just the birds for company.

Halfway through our day's walk we reached San Juan de Ortega, another village existing purely for the Camino trade. The place had a slightly Cotswoldy[1] feel about it, perhaps it was the honey coloured stone. The church and former monastery was said to be built by San Juan [Saint John] himself, a one man whirlwind of a church, bridge and hospital builder from the twelfth century.

Supposedly, a carved frieze depicting the Annunciation is lit by sunlight at six pm each spring and autumn equinox with the holy rays falling on a statue of the Virgin Mary. This is known as the 'miracle of the light'. This phenomenon was only rediscovered in 1974, centuries after the church's construction.

---

[1] An area of rolling hills in south central England.

We reached the Hotel Papasol. We weren't stopping there but had booked into the nearby casa rural. We had definitely decided that these rural houses were more authentic places to stay.

"Do you know where the Casa Rural Papasol is please?" The locals at the bar looked at us in deep thought, hands rubbing chins in contemplation, bewildered looks…

"Sorry, no." Then, "Hang on a moment." said a rather inebriated gentleman at the bar. "Yes, it's the building next door I think." And there it was, directly opposite. We never got to the bottom of whether they were being obtuse, had fallen out with the owners or were genuinely surprised that there was a property with the same name as theirs ten yards across the road.

Our ancestor (I say 'our' when I mean 'Lynne's') with his Bohemian hairstyle and inquisitive look peered out of the line drawing on the municipal sign to Atapuerca. We were about to visit a Neanderthal homestead.

I was not sure we were heading for the visitors' centre or state penitentiary as we approached a stark concrete and gunmetal caged box, its profile jarring against the flat and barren landscape. Whereas museums of old were stuffed full of artifacts, the modern approach is to look suspiciously as if you do not have enough objects to display but have plenty of space for hordes of schoolchildren to run about and eat their sandwiches.

Firstly, we needed context and what better place to start than the papier mâché cave followed by the des res wigwam house with neatly woven wattle walls and feathery fronds upon the roof. I hoped it didn't rain much. And what were these items scattered around the floor? Bones? Human bones?

Yes, it appeared that Mister and Missus Tharg had a penchant for eating each other. Yes, Homo Antecessor was a cannibal. Humans were a 'high-ranked' prey meaning 'a lot of food could be obtained from humans at low cost'. Good to know, as long as you were towards to the top of the food chain. But this was only the experimental archaeology section; we were booked into the actual dining room area of the dig.

The bus created a dust cloud as it travelled the few kilometres to the site. Here we would meet the remains of the earliest humanoids in Europe. This lot turned up about a million years ago and were probably native to Europe, rather than us modern day interlopers who travelled up from Africa.

The dig had discovered a large pit into which animals may well have fallen and humanoids had 'buried' their dead there. I say 'buried', when I perhaps mean tossed down there after the best bits had been chewed off like discarded KFC.

Our guide was a young archaeologist who told us in very good English that she wouldn't be conducting the tour in English. This was a little bit of a shame as it wouldn't have been too much of an imposition to give us a very quick and occasional translation. However, one of the other visitors did help us out when we looked particularly lost. 'Canibalismo' is pretty much the same in any language.

We returned to our rooms for a wash and brush up before revisiting the bar with the geographically challenged regulars, including the even more inebriated gentleman who had finally told us where our accommodation was. Stupidly, we sat next to him.

Our companion was an Anglophile. Queen "good", Prince Charles "useless", Camilla "must have her head chopped off" and Lady Di, pronounced 'lay dee dee', "a saint". Other opinions on all things British were passed including a quick rundown of the best British pop groups, topped by the Beatles and Simon and Garfunkel (obviously the British ones).

Our table couldn't have become vacant soon enough and we bid goodbye to our new friend for life. Human was not on the menu tonight although the pork was a little suspect. As an added bonus, the couple at the table next to us left most of their wine. Well, it would have been churlish not to.

We got lost. Well, it was misty and it wasn't entirely our fault. There were shells and arrows along the way and to all intents and purposes it looked like the correct route. But it wasn't. This was a five kilometre dead end. This was a first for us and we had prided ourselves on keeping to the right path, but now we had to find our way back. This was not as easy as we had hoped. To add to our misfortune, the next section was open moorland; a thousand metres high and the mist was now fog. We wandered lonely in the cloud, suppressing panic.

We had a compass. Somewhere. We rifled through our bags. Perhaps we'd left it at home. That would be it.

The Sierra de Atapuerca was only 25 square kilometres, so as long as we kept walking in the general direction we thought we should be going, in a pea souper, we were bound to find the path eventually …

Soft focus figures formed in the distance, we headed towards them and they soon took human form. We followed the humanoids and suddenly here were the reassuring arrows and shells. So much different from the false ones we'd been tempted to follow hours beforehand.

Abruptly the moorland ended and we were in the suburbs of Burgos. The Cardeñuela Riopico café provided us with coffee and custard doughnuts (custard now being part of our five a day). There was money here. The houses had gates and alarms and signs telling us to be beware of the perros.

We got lost again.

This was becoming a bit of a habit. The 'official' route follows the N-120 which is pretty awful. An alternative route followed the river into a country park that looked lovely. Somehow, we managed to follow the least attractive option, a stroll down the N-1; the Madrid to France highway. Highlights were the airport, railway station and the kilometre long Bridgestone tyre factory. If you were into reinforced concrete or perhaps a university geography student undertaking your *'the decline of the industrial economy in a post modern society'* dissertation, then this was the place for you. For us pilgrims it was a long trudge through very depressing, crumbling suburbs full of smashed glass, graffiti covered, ex plumbing supply warehouses.

After getting lost twice we were determined not to do so again. A challenge in a city that doggedly refused to put up any signage at all. Pilgrims meandered, heads swivelling from side to side, looking for clues on walls, perhaps a flash of yellow paint peeling on a street corner or a scallop scratched onto a bin. We headed for the dirty great spire that was the cathedral.

We had visited Burgos Cathedral when Lynne and I came here a decade ago and therefore I forewent paying seven euros to see it all again. The other thing I remembered from that past trip was that El Cid came from near here.

The Cid, meaning lord or master, was in fact named Rodrigo Díaz de Vivar and was a minor noble in the court King Ferdinand the Great in the latter half of the eleventh century. El Cid worked his way up the slippery slope of the military in a convoluted world of sibling fighting sibling, province fighting province. Ultimately, he found himself on the wrong side and was sent into exile. Here he became a jobbing mercenary fighting for the Muslim rulers of Zaragoza. He returned to the Christian fold and became the ruler of Valencia where he was a well-liked sovereign by Christians and Muslims alike.

He continued scrapping with the Berbers of north Africa until his death when he became Charlton Heston and had a broomstick stuck up his jerkin to lead his troops into battle one last time[1]. Unfortunately, this bit was just a Hollywood myth and he most likely died from famine as a result of a siege on Valencia.

Jacotrans had delivered Lynne's rucksack to the Hotel Norte Y Londres so we knew we were in the right place. However, the bag sat in an opulent marbled foyer. Far to posh for us dishevelled pilgrims - surely? This was a grand Victorian hotel with high ceilings, spacious rooms and creaky floors. Again, we thought (briefly) about our fellow travellers fighting for a bed in the municipal auberge.

We weren't looking for a bar with the world's most miserable waitress but somehow we found it. We had city-wide Wi-Fi so I typed in 'Why are Spanish waiters so miserable?' There were 9,140,000 results. Okay, they're not paid particularly well, but if they are going to rely on tips then they are probably going the wrong way about it.

I also searched for 'Tapas bars near here?' TripAdvisor recommended a tapas bar close to the hotel, La Favorita. Chalk and

---

[1] 1961 epic historical drama directed by Anthony Mann. The film ends with the very dead El Cid being strapped to his horse and paraded before his troops, the narrator proclaiming: "And thus the Cid rode out of the gates of history into legend."

cheese when it came to serving staff. Here the black-uniformed waiters were pleasant, welcoming and helpful.

"Fifteen hundred euros a kilo." the waiter told us the angulas (elvers) went for. "More than gold." The ones in front of us were a couple of euros. "These are fake", he continued, "made from shredded fish, but very nice." And they were too.

We asked our friendly barman if he could recommend a wine to go with the tapas. I wanted a robust red and Lynne a local white. The barman said that whilst the wines on the blackboard were nice, he had some specials from under the counter. Here goes I thought ...

These were lovely, from the Ribera del Duero; mine a deep claret colour, peppery and spicy; the sort of wine that you could stand a teaspoon up in. Lynne went for the Albariño, a bit more gutsy than a Sauvignon Blanc and with a peachy, tropical fruit nose and taste. We had a couple.

We needed sleep and returned for a siesta.

Now for the evening's entertainment. We could have been anywhere in the world. Craft beer bars attract the same clientele, have the same décor and the same handwriting on a chalkboard describing the beers. The *Golden Rock and Beer* also came with heavy metal and biker leathers. People shouted at each other. Coals to Newcastle came to mind as the barman served me a hoppy IPA from Dyce in Aberdeen. Then to confuse matters we moved on to the *Dougall's IPA 4* which hailed from Spain.

We bar hopped. We left the pilgrim crowds behind as we moved later and later into the evening. The Spanish came out. We ate with them. We were going to be very tired in the morning.

BURGOS - LEÓN

Bullfighting is still big in Spain. Perhaps there are not quite the number of bars showing it on television as there used to be (whether because it's not now politically correct or the UEFA Champions League's dominates on the entertainment front) but there are still traditional bars that hark back to the heyday of the 'corrida de toros', and the Taberna Casa Comidas, our breakfast stop, was one such.

Akin to a small English pub, the bar was cosy, dark, with exposed beams. Bullfighting memorabilia festooned the walls including a tiled wall depicting all the different types of bulls used in the ring. Apart from the television in the corner, nothing had changed for half a century and we half expected to see Ernest Hemingway walk in at any moment. A taciturn barman served us our coffee and croissant, well it was early, and he'd probably only had a few hours' sleep, as had we.

We had time on our hands as we'd planned two nights in Burgos but decided that we would only stay one. The Museum of Human Evolution was an obvious choice of morning entertainment and there was a pilgrim discount. We dodged schoolchildren running riot in the airy museum halls and headed to the Gallery of Hominids. Lucy (Australopithecus) was there, as were Homo Neanderthalensis, Homo Heidelbergensis and, of course, us, Homo Sapiens. Whilst I was interested in how we humans came about, the children around us were more interested in the models' furry genitalia, which is exactly how we humans came about.

Starting out at midday meant we had missed all the pilgrim traffic and the route out of Burgos was much nicer than that coming in, the suburbs surrounded by parks and municipal green areas.

Rabé de las Calzadas was a sleepy hamlet of 150 souls, pretty rich ones looking at the houses as we entered the village. The proprietor of our hostal greeted us warmly and gave us both a Miraculous Medal portraying an image of the Virgin Mary tied on with a piece of red thread. We were honoured. We had no idea what it was or what to do with it, but it was a nice touch. I tied mine on to the back of my rucksack. That'd keep the devil from sneaking up on me.

We knew things were just about to go wrong when two Irishmen, Roger and Michael, joined us for a beer before dinner. Michael was a font of all Camino knowledge, having worked at an albergue on the northern route for a few weeks. Roger knew how to drink.

Sausage (morcilla), egg and chips were on the menu. Well, it wasn't quite the bangers we got at home, more like black pudding, but it provided much needed sustenance and would hopefully soak up some of the alcohol. It didn't.

Back in the room we found that the toilet wouldn't work. Unfortunately, this was only after Lynne had deposited her morcilla; not something I was looking forward to being reunited with in the morning.

My Swiss Army knife and a bit of lateral thinking had temporarily mended the toilet, although I'd probably need to sterilise the knife when I next had a kettle in my room. Note to self, always boil room kettle once before making tea. I felt obliged to inform the proprietor about the flush problem and strung together a 17 word sentence. Thanks Lander, all those lessons were worth it. I'm not sure the proprietor understood a word of what I said, but he nodded politely.

Today we were entering the Meseta.

The Meseta is a large expanse of very flat plain and we would have to walk through about 200 kilometres of it. The guidebooks and blogs are always very dismissive of this part of the path, usually stating that it is monotonous, dull and boring. Some pilgrims even avoid this section. Given that this walk is a pilgrimage and something of a challenge, it all seemed a bit of a cop-out and my view was that such pilgrims should not get a full Compostela[1].

If there was going to be one issue it was going to be the lack of shade. This was not a problem for us in April, but would probably be more of a concern it you were walking this in the heat of the summer.

Whilst this area had its drawbacks, it was flat, and you could get a good number of kilometres under your belt reasonably quickly. It was here that we bumped into Matt, who we had last seen at the Alto del Perdón with his father. Matt told us he'd 'lost' his father and we were quite concerned that he'd died en route, only to be informed that the father had had to give up and had flown back home to England.

Romilly was very religious. We'd not met many overt believers en route or, if we had, they'd not mentioned the fact. Romilly was keen to let us know and was limping badly. For someone who had such faith, her life continued to deal her a pretty crap hand or, in this case, foot. However, help was at … foot as the next stop and her overnight accommodation, San Bol, had a well where the waters supposedly cured sore feet. Good luck to her. We'd stick to Compeed blister patches and our Miraculous Medal.

Waiting in the wings was our next travelling companion. Sometimes you never quite get around to asking people's names. On this occasion we didn't need to. His name was Mister Know-it-all from Canberra, Australia.

Mr KIA was a seasoned pilgrim and could tell you everything about the Camino: the area we were travelling through, what the weather was going to do, the best places to stay, the best weight for a rucksack (15 kilos) and a host of other tedious information. I didn't really take to him and so we walked a bit slower to let him stride off ahead at precisely the right speed (4.728 km/hour).

We passed the church and albergue at San Bol. It looked pretty basic and I'd heard that it had no electricity or sanitation. One on-line reviewer suggested San Bol was for the '*sweet, earthy, touchy-feely, artistic type pilgrim*'. Romilly would probably be in her element.

---

[1] Official certificate of completion.

Having said that the Meseta was flat and we could see for ever, it was therefore a bit of a surprise when Hontanas suddenly appeared from nowhere in a bit of a dip, its Romanesque church tower rising up from the centre of tightly packed low level red roofs.

The village square offered a choice of seating: '¿Sol y Sombra?' Sun or shade? It wasn't quite clear which bar served which tables, especially as many pilgrims had played solar musical chairs before we had arrived. Whatever, we managed to get a beer and bocadillo stuffed full of eggy tortilla. We opted for sun.

Now to find our accommodation, somewhere with indoor facilities would be good. We'd booked in advance but nothing in the village had the right name. We knew the place must exist as Lynne's rucksack was not in any of the bars. In the end we asked a local bar owner and he provided a key to the small casa rural across the street.

All that a pilgrim needs in their room are a few hooks to hang up damp clothing and a bit of space to place a rucksack. Our room had neither. Not even a shelf to place a toothbrush. It did, however, have a very strong odour of lavender – that should deter the bed bugs.

The pilgrim locusts had denuded the menu by the time Lynne, Matt (he of the father that wasn't dead) and I sat down for the later sitting. I'd enjoyed the morcilla, egg and chips the night before, so I had them again. I looked up morcilla in my electronic dictionary and was told it was a Spanish black pudding, made with pigs' blood, flash boiled to coagulate the said blood and then cured. This was my sort of meal. I hoped the toilet worked.

No fresh bed bug bites. The lavender had obviously done its job. It had certainly ravaged my nasal passages, so much so that I had no sense of smell whatsoever, save that I kept thinking that I was outside a branch of Lush, you know, the British cosmetics retailer that smells so awful to let blind people know to avoid it.

A problem presented itself. Here in Hontanas there were supposedly 160 bed spaces (although I was not sure where they were all hidden). In Itero, our next stop, there were just 60 and given that many pilgrims would be walking the same full day as us (about 19 kilometres) there may well be a bit of a log-jam. Pre-booking was on the cards. I plucked up courage and dialled a number from the guide.

I had scribbled down what I needed to say on a napkin, all phonetically detailed, lest I stumbled over any word. I stumbled over all of them but, at the end of the spiel, I was quite pleased with myself. The recipient of my call listened patiently. "English." He said and put down the phone. Well, that was successful. I now had no idea whether we had a booking or whether the gentleman put the phone down in exasperation.

Ethereal music swarmed around the ancient carcass of the Arco de San Antón, it put me in mind of Enya[1] on benzodiazepine[2]. The road snaked through this ruined monastery which,  miraculously, had retained its two vaulted arches and pilgrims craned their necks to look up as they passed. The building was once part of the palace of King Pedro I of Castile, no doubt built to save his soul from eternal damnation given that he was also known as Peter the Cruel.

San Antón Abad, to whom the monastery was dedicated, was a somewhat more benevolent character, despite his unfortunate name. Living as a hermit and looking after wildlife in Egypt in the late third century, he became the patron saint of domestic animals. The monks of his order specialised in curing (I use the word reservedly) those suffering from Saint Anthony's Fire, today known as ergotism.

Ergotism was a poisoning caused by a fungus growing on rye grass and then baked into bread. Its symptoms were particularly nasty causing sufferers to go mad followed by gangrene due to lack of blood supply to the extremities. In turn, this caused a burning sensation akin to being burnt at the stake, before your hands and feet dropped off. I

---

[1] Irish singer, songwriter and musician known for her modern. often doleful, Celtic music.
[2] A tranquilizer.

was not sure what the 'cure' was, but given this was a medieval affliction, it was unlikely to be pleasant or effective.

Whilst this was a medieval scourge, the same poisoning reared its ugly head in Salem in America in 1692/3 when children, poisoned by the fungus' LSD-like qualities, accused two hundred local folk of witchcraft, resulting in 19 executions.

An old man had parked a battered van just before the arch and was selling trinkets from a tray. We picked up a couple of 'T' shaped crosses, Tau, which protected wearers from madness and decoupling limbs. We bought a couple and tied them to our rucksacks next to our Miraculous Medals. Best euro spent all day.

A spectacular view of the next village greeted us. Yet another monastery perched on the side of the hill, its slopes terraced for vines, its position looking more military than religious.

Brierley promised a café here at Castrojeriz, and he was not wrong. This was a modern, spacious bar, catering for pilgrims and obviously very successful. The staff were welcoming and efficient, the coffee perfect and the Wi-Fi signal strong. If it had one fault it was the fact that Rick Astley's[1] *Never Gonna Give You Up* was playing over the sound system; oh, and the very ill Frenchman in the toilet who had obviously had one morcilla too many. I washed my hands very thoroughly after visiting and touched my Tau for good luck.

Whilst the café was very twenty-first century, the village convenience store was very much stuck in the 1950s. this was the sort of place that your gran would have visited, all dark wood, small windows and chock full of everything you could ever want; wine, fresh vegetables, snacks, commemorative shells and an eclectic selection of brown clothes originating from 70 years ago. They didn't appear to be second hand and had probably been there, unsold since the shop opened when they were the height of fashion. We bought some hard sheep's cheese for our lunch.

A 12 per cent incline is not what you expect in the Meseta, but here it was and we would have to climb the Alto de Mostelares to get to our next destination. Swarms of lycra-clad Italian cyclists, were on a

---

[1] English singer, songwriter with a string of hits in the 1980s.

mission to get to the top as well, pedestrian pilgrims a minor inconvenience as they scooted by us with millimetres to spare, their little bells tinkling ineffectually.

At the top the Italians were lounged around the seating area. I was tempted to issue a cutting rebuke to them about manners, but castigating them would have been like telling off a naughty puppy; the moment had passed and they wouldn't have understood anyway.

At the other side of the wide plateau we were greeted by a magnificent view, the Meseta in all its billiard table glory, majestic in its silence. We soaked up the moment and then … *"Never gonna give you up, never gonna let you down"* interrupted the earworm. Damn you Stock, Aitken and Waterman[1]. Damn you.

Down was no easier than up and we were again accosted by the iridescent Italians as they careered towards the bottom of the plain. Hopefully, someone further down would stick a walking pole in one of their front spokes.

The Tierra de Campos was a vast green plain, a rich and fertile patchwork of fields growing everything from vegetables, wheat and vines. One particular crop in abundance was a pea-green small leaved plant. I asked a friendly looking farmer what it was. He said it was alfalfa for the cows. Well, that's what I think he said.

All that was required was to put one foot in front of the other, my mind slipped into neutral. Perhaps this was a form of mindfulness, the cares of the world forgotten, not that I had many to start with.

Like a bored and irascible child a Camino direction sign had scrawled upon it *'Are we there yet?'* It made me smile. I took a photograph.

An albergue described in many of the guidebooks as the 'authentic Camino experience' passed by. No electricity, lit by candlelight and a rustic toilet and shower in the garden were its selling points. Here monks would wash your feet and take care of your spiritual needs. Singing *Kumbaya* was obligatory before dinner. The Ermita de San Nicolás didn't appeal.

---

[1] English songwriting and record production trio who wrote and produced the song.

We reached our accommodation. The owner stood behind the bar drying glasses.

"Llamé por teléfono." I mimed holding a phone to my ear.

"El inglés?" said the owner.

"Sí." I was definitely getting the hang of the lingo.

We used the outside washing area to give our walking gear a freshen up. I had purchased a set of fluorescent quick drying walking underpants for the trip: yellow, lime green and orange. I hung them up on the line. No one would mistakenly take these.

With both clothes and ourselves clean we ambled into town to see what delights were on offer. There were few. An airy bar drew us in and we sat at the counter and ordered a couple of large beers. A fellow pilgrim entered and sat next to us. He too ordered a large beer. We introduced ourselves and he asked if we had any particular reason for walking the route.

"We're on a long walk." said I.

"I've had some medical issues." responded Raymond.

Raymond had been rebuilt. If we had been playing *Top Trumps[1]*, he would have beaten me hands down in every category. Imagine a cross between the Bionic Man and Robocop[2]. Raymond was a walking titanium endoskeleton. I was impressed.

Raymond was also South African and, in the spirit of the Camino, I forgave him for that. The conversation and the beer flowed until Lynne reminded me that we needed to eat and Raymond, reluctantly said he too should rejoin his wife and do the same.

A pan-European Esperanto was the lingua franca for the rest of the evening. The owner had placed us at a table with two German women. They spoke no English and my German was limited to second world war films which I thought may have been inappropriate. All of us had some appalling French and the table cloth was white paper, so with sign language and poorly drawn diagrams and maps we spent a lovely two hours not understanding each other.

---

[1] Whist-like card game.
[2] The Six Million Dollar Man, American science fiction and action television series, running from 1973 to 1978 and Robocop, 1987 American science fiction action film and later franchise.

84

A Basil/Sybilesque[1] argument broke out in the kitchen. I was wondering whether we could get a little more wine but was afraid to ask. When 'Basil' stormed out, I sheepishly indicated that we could do with a drop more. He came back, plonked a new, full bottle on the table and went back to continue the argument. It was a great evening.

The second bottle had taken its toll on Lynne and we were pleased to have a short day ahead. Two Swedes walked with us. We discussed *Downton Abbey*[2]. None of us had actually seen the programme, but that didn't stop us chatting amiably for an hour or so about it.

The Canal de Castilla made for pleasant walking with its noisy corncrakes and reed warblers. This was a very different Camino from that which we were used to and we could have been in the Norfolk Broads[3], something which the authorities hoped to emulate when the canal was restored to its navigable roots.

It had been threatening to rain all morning, and as we entered Frómista the heavens opened. Perfect timing for once as we had just reached the foyer of our accommodation.

Our hotel promised all modern amenities. Give it its due, it was modern, although the amenities left a little to be desired.

Our room reminded me of one of those retro chocolate lime sweets; all green and brown. This was a hotel that was trying to be upmarket but missing the mark at every step. On examining the bathroom complimentary toiletries, I had the suspicion that the maid had not really given much thought to what the modern pilgrim might want at the end of a long and tiring day. They consisted of three plastic bottles of body lotion and a lip balm. Perhaps it gets dry out here.

Lunch was tapas in a bar opposite the imposing Iglesia de San Martín. Consecrated in the same year that we were being invaded by the French in 1066, this was as fine a Romanesque church as we would see. We didn't go in.

---

[1] Husband and wife characters in the 1970's British situation comedy, Fawlty Towers, set in a south coast seaside hotel.
[2] British historical drama television series set in the early 20th century.
[3] An area of wetlands and navigable rivers and lakes in the English counties of Norfolk and Suffolk.

It took quite a bit of ah-humming at dinner to get the attention of the waitress in the hotel dining room, mainly because she and the owner were discussing something far more important than serving customers. When the food did arrive, the steak was as tough as a pair of old Camino boots. My guess was that most people staying were pilgrims who were only there for one night. Therefore, it mattered little to the proprietors, chefs and bar staff whether they gave a good service or not. Today they let people down and tomorrow a new set of punters would arrive to be let down also. Such a shame.

A full Brierley today; Frómista to Carrión de los Condes, 20 kilometres. It was also cold and raining. I hadn't really taken to our overnight stop. Probably the church drew too many busloads of tourists and their needs took precedence over pilgrims.

 Where there was a choice of paths along the route you could guarantee that the waymarking would be lacking or non-existent. However, today we were following the P-980, a dead straight road with adjacent pathway, the Pilgrim Senda or pilgrim motorway. There was no way we would get lost. Therefore, the route had dozens upon dozens of signs pointing the way. More atrocious service was had at the €2.85 breakfast stop. Perhaps the price should have forewarned me. This is my view on life. If you are offering a service, then provide that service. If you do not want to, don't advertise. At least the place was warm with a log burner pumping out solar core type temperatures. We dried off quickly. However, we were going to get wet again.

The weather forecast on the television was depressing. Rain, and plenty of it with pictures of flooded rivers and interviews with depressed looking hoteliers saying they were 85 percent down on the previous year. Well, it was a bank holiday weekend. What else would you expect.

Whilst it was occasionally wet, we got into stride with Tom from Aberdeen who was a retired oil engineer. Again, the miles melted away once you got into conversation and the pelting rain a mere inconvenience.

Having had little interest in the hundreds of religious buildings we had passed, there is nothing like a twelfth century church when it's pouring with rain. Villalcázar de Sirga had one of these and we were grateful for a respite from the atrocious weather outdoors. 900 years ago white robed Templars would have been walking along the church's long thin aisle, perhaps bathed in the same kaleidoscopic colours from the stained glass windows.

Yet another classic photo opportunity presented itself outside the church. A bronze statue of a seated pilgrim in full medieval garb enjoying a jug of wine. A spare chair stood next to him and there cannot be one pilgrim who had not taken advantage of this tableau.

Two young, female Danish volunteers located accommodation for us at the tourist information office at Carrión de los Condes. The Spanish pilgrim behind us was not so fortunate.

Walking the Camino had its challenges, but walking with a dog as well, on a bank holiday, was a step too far, even if there were fourteen albergues in the town. I stroked the dog and commiserated with the chap who looked a bit like Joe Wicks[1] with his tousled, wavey dark locks. The next village of any size was another five miles away and the weather was getting worse and, of course, there was no guarantee of accommodation there either. Hailstones the size of marbles pelted down creating an instant white carpet as we ran to our hostal.

Whilst we had been reliant on our Brierley to get us from A to B, previous pilgrims had used guides since the dawn of the Camino, a

---

[1] Aka 'the Body Coach'. British fitness coach, TV presenter, social media personality and author.

thousand years ago. One of these was the *Codex Calixtinus*, written in the early to mid-twelfth century. No medieval pilgrim traveller wanting to follow the way of Saint James should be without it. Like Brierley, it contained religious instruction, sermons, useful holy texts to read, details of Saint James and his miracles and helpful day to day advice to pilgrims. This passage describes the people of Gascony:

"When you've crossed this place, you come to Gascony, with its white bread and the best and reddest wine, and plenty of forests, streams, meadows and healthy fountains. And the people? Fast-talking, obnoxious, and sex-crazed, they are overfed, poorly-dressed drunks. They've two good characteristics: they are skilled warriors, and they give good hospitality to the poor."

The *Codex Calixtinus* says that Carrión de los Condes was '*rich in bread and wine*' and after the hail had stopped we avoided the lake sized puddles to explore the town and seek some of that famous bread and wine.

The town was the de facto capital of the Meseta. Originally ruled by a noble family, the Banu Gómezes, a dysfunctional and, by all accounts, not very nice group of individuals. Two of this familly married and then, unwisely, mistreated a couple of the daughters of El Cid, by beating them and then abandoning them in a forest to be eaten by wolves. The Cid, a little peeved at this, dispatched the two husbands as punishment.

We had a quick look in the Romanesque church of Santa María del Camino dedicated to the Virgin of Victory (to celebrate a Spanish victory in Cyprus in 1571). A frieze depicted the tribute demanded by the Muslim emirate of Córdoba of one hundred maidens as a peace treaty after defeating the Spanish in the late seven hundreds. The maidens were to be half of noble birth, the other half, commoners. Variety was obviously the spice of life.

A very loud television echoed around the lunchtime bar but the tapas was very good as was the Wi-Fi signal. We were searching for accommodation for the following day. We found a couple of bunks in a dormitory in the next town at the extortionate price of 20 euros each!

There were plenty of places to eat in the evening and we chose a busy restaurant attached to one of the albergues. At the table next to us sat three American women. Listening into their conversation it went like this:

"Do you have vegetarian food?"

"Yes. We have Russian salad." said the waiter.

"Doesn't that contain tuna?"

"Yes."

"Tuna is not a vegetable."

"Yes it is."

One then went on to say she couldn't eat tomatoes or peppers and they were also tee-total. Some people were going to find the Camino very challenging.

I had the Russian salad which did, indeed, contain tuna. Lynne had potatoes and chorizo. Mains were gammon and chips followed by a plastic tubbed chocolate cream pudding which listed as its main ingredients; starch and glucose – no mention of chocolate or cream. All of this washed down with a passable local tempranillo.

The restaurant was buzzing, full to the gunnels with pilgrims sharing tables, food and conversation. Everyone was enjoying themselves apart from the women next to us, one of whom was picking out the tomatoes, peppers and bits of tuna from her salad.

Tom, the engineer from Aberdeen, was in the restaurant and we left together in search of a bar for a late-night beer. We had one and then another which, for some inexplicable reason, the bar did not charge us. We tried, in our best Spanish, to explain but they were adamant that we had paid for it. In the end we gave them a five euro tip, for which they were very grateful, although perhaps not when they cashed up for the night and found the till ten euros short.

If we wanted two bunks together, we needed to get off early. The scent of freshly baked bread guided us to the panaderia and we picked up a couple of pains aux raisins. It wasn't raining. That was a bonus. Weak sunlight warmed and misted the ground as we walked along the old Roman road, stopping to devour our still warm bready breakfast along the way.

The road was straight (well it was Roman) and one kilometre was very much the same as the last. To our north we could see the snow topped peaks of Los Picos de Europa, a 20 kilometre strip of mountains forming part of the Cantabrian range.

A ramshackle collection of primary coloured plastic chairs was the Café Oasis, Descanso Rest area. Plastic beakers of coffee fortified us as we made good progress to Calzadilla de la Cueza and would head the queue at our albergue.

We arrived at the stroke of midday. The albergue was closed. We camped out in a bar opposite so we could keep an eye on the door. Joe Wicks and his dog turned up and we asked him how he had fared the night before.

"I cooked the Danish girls a Spanish omelette and they let me sleep with them." I didn't enquire further.

The door to the albergue shuddered open and, like a shot, we were there. It transpired that we had not just booked two bunks, but the entire dormitory. Result. Even more so as I had developed a touch of 'Santiago's Revenge' and decided that a long nap was needed, close to a toilet. The only thing to do now was decide which bunk to sleep in.

By evening time my stomach had settled down and we joined a crowd in the minuscule restaurant attached to our albergue. Raymond and Barbara from South Africa poked their head in and we made room for them, then a couple of Canadians and a lone Portuguese chap. It was all very cosy.

The owners were Canarian and the menu had a slight north African twist to it. The lemon chicken and Canarian potatoes were particularly authentic.

Raymond and I spat out our wine in unison. It was disgusting. We donated the bottles to the other end of the table and invested in a bottle of Valencian Reserva. Things went a bit awry afterwards.

It started with a round of Spanish brandies (the mothers' milk variety), then the local pacharán (much more aniseedy than previously) and then café con leche con leche, a Canarian concoction of coffee, condensed milk and Licor Cuarenta y Tres (43), an ancient digestive made from fruit and herbs.

As we left the bar our companions said they wanted to be up at six the following morning. Somehow, I doubted they would be fit enough.

I then looked at my watch. Ten pm. Curfew at the municipal albergue, down the road, was nine pm. Oh dear.

I fell into a fitful sleep with some pretty weird dreams. One involved Christine Lagarde, the Managing Director of the International Monetary Fund. Best to keep off the Cuarenta y Tres in the future.

Up bright and early, which came as a bit of a surprise, and we were soon on the road. After six kilometres we stopped for a protein and carbohydrate filled tortilla and coffee. We met up with the group from last night who had not got off at six as planned, nor did they look particularly bright.

Ledigos, Terradillos de los Templarios, Moratinos, San Nicolás del Real Camino; a steady stream of tiny Templar hamlets broke up the monotony of a dead straight N-120. At Moratinos we came across a number of small bricked entrances burrowed into the hillsides. These were 'bodegas' and were originally used to store food and wine, going back to Roman times. These bodegas were dug as a 'pastime' by children who were kept warm and out of mischief in the winter months. Tell that to kids today and they wouldn't believe you. Today, these 'Hobbit houses' (as they were described on the information board) were used as mini holiday homes. One even had a television aerial sticking out from the top.

A pair of maroon checked carpet slippers strode out in front of us, followed by a Jack Russell. Here we were: Gore-Tex boots, Compeed plasters, silk lined socks, and the locals walk three kilometres to the nearest bar in their slippers. We followed him to the bar for our pre-lunchtime beer and free ham tapas (which the resident cat ate). He didn't appear to be suffering from any blisters.

The church at San Nicolás de Real Camino had its own pelota court. Pelota is played with a rubber ball and a little bat against a wall, a bit like squash, although there are other versions using gloves, like fives[1], or a scoop or net which speeds up the ball. All versions are very fast moving and potentially lethal.

The Camino crossed into the province of León at a confluence of motorway crash barriers. Not a pretty sight, but very safe, as long as you were on the right side of them, given the speed of the maniacal Spanish drivers.

Railway lines guided us into Sahagún and we were on the wrong side of them. An aura of decay permeated the buildings we passed by: windows boarded, roofs collapsed, concrete cancer sprouting fledgling trees. A wheat storage warehouse, standing like a cathedral, was crumbling before our very eyes and the bullring, wallpapered with tattered posters, suggested the last bull to be killed would have been eaten many years ago. I half expected a swarm of zombies to appear from the post-apocalyptic ruination.

In amongst the dereliction stood an attempt at regeneration; a red bricked hotel, imaginatively called 'Hotel'. Flags of all nations limply identified this as an 'international' hotel, the sort of place where reception would have Madrid, London and New York clocks. It didn't look very inviting.

First stop, the town's central albergue to pick up Lynne's rucksack. I reminded her that she was missing out on the full Camino experience, but it didn't seem to worry her. Next a very English looking pub, all dark wood, curved bar, fruit machine[2] in the corner and four craft ales. We tried all four.

We'd pre-booked accommodation at the Hotel Puerto de Sahagún and located it on the municipal map in a handy square… ah it was the 'Hotel' hotel. Why on earth didn't it have its name on the outside? We trudged back through the post-apocalyptic entrance to the town.

As expected the hotel was of the modern 'conference' style: airy lobby, staff in uniforms, efficient booking in, clocks telling the time around the world. It was, however, devoid of guests and later we found

---

[1] An English sport played with gloved hands, mainly at very prestige public (private) schools.
[2] British term for a gambling machine that creates a game of chance.

also devoid of Wi-Fi and hot water. But, hey, we were pilgrims and could cope with that, and it was dirt cheap.

A restaurant had been recommended to us, El Ruedo, and that was where we were heading for our evening meal. It wasn't pilgrim friendly, by which I mean that it didn't open at six o'clock and have macaroni on the menu.

A few headscarfed, elderly women in black sat on benches. They looked as if they'd been there since the 1950s. Children played in the square, chasing each other on their bikes. This was a town just waking up from both an afternoon siesta and from a long winter, with the bare vines just starting to green ready to crawl along the pre-strung wires and to keep the summer sun off when it came later in the year.

Sahagún had once been prosperous, the railway lines evidencing much commercial activity, but now it all looked outdated, perhaps its only industry now was that of pilgrims passing through. In one corner of the square stood a shoe shop, the sort of shop with a bay window and yellow cellophane to keep out the sun. In the window were a row of walking boots, no doubt for the weary pilgrim in need of new footwear. And, in the middle of this display, pairs of carpet slippers in exactly the same colour and style as we had seen the old farmer wearing earlier in the day!

We decided to stake out the restaurant from a bar opposite. Again, it had a slightly English feel to it, with its dark wooded bar and mid-twentieth century décor. The owner was reserved, a man of few words. The beers were diverse and the tapas substantial: gammon and bread, whitebait, squid and olives. If we were not careful, we would peak too early.

Despite its 8.30pm opening, the restaurant did have a pilgrims' menu. However, we had been looking forward to something a bit special: baby caramelised leeks with foie gras followed by roasted leg of milk fed lamb, carved at the table. To say this was 'perfecto' would have been an understatement (in fact it was so good we asked the friendly red shirted waiter to take a very blurred photo of us eating it). The meat fell off the bone and melted in the mouth, slow cooked all day no doubt. We washed this down with a local wine; deep red, the colour of arterial blood with dark chocolate, liquorice and leather somewhere in the mix. All of this was topped off with a 'carafe' – yes, you heard correctly, a carafe of brandy. We were not sure whether it was all for us, but it was. This time Lynne took a very blurred photo of me drinking the carafe. I have come to the conclusion that it may not be the photographer that was at fault! The bill came to 70 euros not bad for one of the best meals we'd had so far.

We lurched back to our hotel, following the railway line and into the deserted hotel with its ultra-efficient but completely under-employed reception staff wishing us a good night.

Sahagún marked the half way point of the walk from St Jean. Lynne had decided to have a rest day. Whether this was prompted by the still full stomach and blood alcohol levels from the night before, or just a touch of 'tiredness' I didn't know. I therefore set off alone to be waved off by the morning's thumb twiddling staff.

Barely awake pilgrims stopped for coffee in the centre of town. I joined them. I sat down for a bun and coffee and chatted to Michael, a South African and his two companions that I had briefly walked with yesterday. They had decided that the next section was too hard/boring/long and planned to take the train to León rather than continue to walk in the Meseta. The word 'cheat' came to mind and I made a mental note to let the Pilgrims' Office in Santiago know.

Infused with caffeine and blood sugar brimming with simple carbohydrates, I set off out of town and immediately met up with the Six Million Rand Raymond and his wife, Barbara. We spent the day together, walking all the way with them to El Burgo Ranero. Raymond and I put the world to rights over the hours, mainly talking about viniculture and how cheap a bottle of good red wine was in South Africa.

Lynne had decided to take a taxi from the hotel although those very nice and efficient people at Jacotrans had popped into the hotel, just in case she had forgotten to let them know about a luggage transfer.

I approached El Burgo along a road of cut wheat with a few remote farm buildings dotted along the horizon, to enter uninspiring suburbs which continued into an uninspiring town centre. Lynne had ensconced herself in a small bar, so insignificant that I had walked past it and it took quite a while for us to find each other.

As was traditional, arriving pilgrims would meet for a drink as soon as their bags had been dumped by the side of their beds, remembering not to put them on top lest the bedbugs crawl in. We sat drinking cold lagers swapping stories with, Ida, an ex-army Dutch woman which included a very untactful conversation about Fawlty Towers and not mentioning the war[1]. Raymond was in his element, also having been in the army. What was astounding was that both the South Africans and Dutch could recite British comedy classics word for word, together with very non-PC funny walk.

Lynne had secured a rather whimsical albergue built by the same designers that had put up post war British holiday camps. Not only that, it also smelled like a 1960's Pontins[2]; a sort of mixture of bleach and lavender scented floor polish. I half expected a Tannoy announcement inviting me to partake in a knobbly knees' competition. No doubt Raymond and Ida would be an expert on Hi-de-Hi[3] as well.

The location was idyllic. Looking out of the window we faced an inland lake, the sun slowly sinking on the horizon, projecting a plum-coloured hue onto the fair weather cumulus clouds in the milky pale blue sky.

Beautiful though it looked, a thought struck me; it was likely we would be bitten to death by the local mosquitos later that night. I would keep the window closed.

Lynne managed to relocate the bar (after a few attempts) she had sat in at lunchtime and we tucked into home made croquetas for starter and a local 'carne guisada' for mains. This was a deeply rich meat and potato stew. The locals were eating the same sauce without meat, but with chunks of tortilla in it. Ice cream with hot caramel sauce, coffee and a bucket of brandy rounded off our evening and we returned back to the albergue with three minutes to spare by the light of a huge full moon.

---

[1]This episode, *The Germans*, contains inappropriate comments about the Second World War.
[2] British company operating holiday parks in the UK, founded in 1946 by Fred Pontin.
[3] British TV sitcom based in a 1950s holiday camp.

We were awoken by three chimes on the camp's xylophone[1]. Only joking. No, we awoke and found that our prudence had paid off and we had not been attacked by mosquitos. The main reason for this may have been that the local and (very) vocal frogs, that had kept us awake for most of the night, had probably eaten them.

With a sporadic Wi-Fi signal we looked for accommodation at our next destination, Mansilla de las Mulas, 'hands on the saddle of the mules'. Nothing stood out and we decided to take our chances when we arrived. Jacotrans were instructed to take Lynne's bag to the municipal albergue and we would take it from there.

I calculated how much the UK were contributing to the EU budget as I crossed a footbridge over a brand new motorway. As I peered over the edge, Kieran from Ireland, did the same.

"I was here a couple of years ago." He started. "There was no traffic on it then." Either the road had still not been commissioned or so little traffic used it as to make it pointless. [As I type this part of the book, I searched Google Maps and placing the little yellow man onto the motorway I counted exactly one car on it!]

Kieran told me he was a tax accountant. We didn't talk much.

Scrubby brown fields accompanied us on our walk all morning, but again it was flat and the kilometres melted away. At Reliegos we stopped at a roadside café festooned with red plastic chairs and tables and a lively hoard of pilgrims (La Cantina de Teddy). It was only six or so kilometres to our overnight stop, so we had plenty of time to sit and chat. Having said that, if we had known what was just up the road, we would have sped up a bit.

---

[1] Another reference to Hi-de-Hi.

I'm not sure Brierley is much of a rocker. If he was, then he would have made more of the next destination, just a few hundred metres from Teddy.

The Elvis Bar (Bar Torre) is a must see along the route. No blog, book or Facebook diary would be complete without a reference to this place. Bright electric turquoise blue, the outside wall was covered in graffiti inspired by a five year old with learning difficulties. Large red letters scrawled on the wall informed us that 'We spak Englis'. On the basis that we 'No spak Español' we would get on like a house on fire.

The Eagles'[1] *Hotel California* blasted from the speakers. The inside was decorated in a similar style to the garish outside, apart from the fact that the five year old's younger brother was in charge of the paint. Every square centimetre of the white plastered wall contained a felt tip message from the thousands of pilgrims passing through.

The mustachio'd and wild bearded, beret wearing owner welcomed us in with a wave of his suspect cigarette.

"Come in."

We ordered beer and Mr Elvis carved off a few slices of jamón Ibérico, adding a little ash to add to the already smoky flavour. *Hotel California* ended and then started again. We ate the ham to be polite although we were not entirely sure that it would pass rigid UK environmental health standards, nor be entirely legal with the added ash. Hopefully, the beer would kill off any bugs.

We wandered, reading the walls. In thousands of years' time, this would be the cave art of our era and future palaeontologists would try

---

[1] American rock band formed in Los Angeles in 1971.

to fathom out what sort of people we were – perhaps whimsical philosophers would describe us best.

Hotel California ended and then started again. I could have stayed there all afternoon but even I was beginning to tire of the '*warm smell of colitas*[1]' repeated every six and a half minutes.

The medieval walls of Mansilla de las Mulas self-limited the available accommodation which was crammed into each and every corner of the town. The municipal albergue looked a little too rustic, so Lynne picked up her bag and we continued our search. The next hostal was full and the third, over a busy bar looked a good bet. The proprietor was a little surly and a woman of few words but with 45 euros in cash handed over (and quickly pocketed) we had a bed for the night. If we'd seen the TripAdvisor reviews in advance, we probably wouldn't have booked in – '*Our worst stay on the Camino*' was the top one.

The room was rather 'basic' and a conversation took place as to whether we should sleep in our permethrin impregnated sleeping bags. However, on inspecting the sheets, they looked clean enough, if not a little old, and the bathroom was serviceable in the way that a hose and bucket would clean you if no other alternative was available.

This was not a room in which we wanted to spend too many waking hours so we popped out immediately for a beer in a delightful little orchard in a parallel road before heading back for a mid afternoon siesta. We would have slept had it not been for a pop-up bar opening directly opposite our window. The laughter and occasional shouting were enough to make sleep difficult, but then, a local Caruso[2] started singing hits from Italian operas. He was remarkably good and we were happy to lay back and listen to him.

Like many towns along the route, we found that they were well provisioned when it came to banks (a half dozen of them) but not so well provisioned when it came to bars and places to eat. Obviously, pilgrims needed cash more than food. We had decided not to eat in the hotel as it looked rather brown and orange and the hosts were still eyeing us with suspicion and disdain, so we wandered the streets.

---

[1] Tip of the marijuana branch.
[2] After Enrico Caruso 1873 –1921, Italian operatic tenor.

We really couldn't face another pilgrim menu but stumbled across a likely looking place just round the corner, La Curiosa. This had trendy written all over it with a downstairs bar lit by recessed wine bottles on shelves in alcoves behind the counter. The bar staff were hipster coiffured (funny haircuts and bushy beards) but very friendly. We had a couple of beers before being shown upstairs to a homely dining room laid with white table cloths and napkins.

Starter was short spaghetti with blue cheese, walnuts and herbs, followed by pescado a la espalda (baked salmon with paprika dusted boiled potatoes). For dessert there was a lemon posset. All very up market by all accounts. Wine was a Lamaciña, Bierzo Mencia which was drinkable although nothing to write home about. For a nightcap we headed back to the lunchtime venue for brandy which we hoped would anesthetise us and kill anything that tried to bite us overnight.

The pop-up bar kicked out at three in the morning with a final rendition of *Che Gelida Manina*[1]. No bug bites and we were out by seven thirty.

A café would have been nice. The GALP service station perhaps not as nice, but it did do coffee, just enough fuel to get us to the Casa Blanca, a roadside turreted café where warm chocolate croissants were selling like, well, hot cakes.

A graveyard for lost hats and broken boots sat in a piece of waste ground. Lost or discarded items of clothing were not an uncommon sight. It was very easy to forget something, especially sticks and walking poles and pilgrims often divested themselves of clothing as it got warmer. What was beguiling was the number of single boots that we came across. Surely, if a sole had fallen off or fabric torn, the wearer would have dumped both shoes. Perhaps I just had not seen any hopping pilgrims yet.

I had expected a Burgos-like trudge into the city, but the route was varied and very pleasant with a sandy rise affording magnificent views before the descent into León. The suburbs were tidy and the Leónese even provided dog parks for the better class of canine with frequent

---

[1] 'Your Tiny Hand is Frozen', La Bohème, Giacomo Puccini

signs to remind owners to '*retiro mis excrementos*'. Plenty of signage guided us into the centre, again very unlike Burgos which had done its best to disorientate the weary pilgrim.

León comes from its Latin name, 'Castra Legionis', and was originally a Roman military camp from the first century BC. Before that it had been populated by local Iberian tribes whom the Romans had conquered during the Cantabrian and Asturian Wars. Thereafter, it had continually been fought over; with the Visigoths, Muslims and the Spanish themselves staking a claim during the Civil War.

Busy, that was what León was. Busy and cosmopolitan. This had been our longest stretch between cities and I'd forgotten about crowds and anyone else that wasn't walking the Camino. Here were: locals, visitors, businessmen, pilgrims and places where you had to watch your wallet or bag. It was all a bit alien.

We had splashed out on a four star hotel, the sort that had very little character and is ideal for conferences, but had all the amenities that we needed to recuperate for a couple of days, with huge beds and fluffy towels, a hairdryer on the wall and no having to share a bathroom with other smelly pilgrims.

León on a Saturday night was not for the fainthearted. It was heaving with the wide streets thronging with families, friends, pilgrims, often in large groups all promenading in the balmy evening air; air full of sounds from street musicians and the whiff of fried foods. There was also another scent, that of malt.

The Cazurra Brew Pub had been brewing and the smell of malt was a siren aroma that was impossible to ignore. The interior was an '*environment with the most elaborate and exclusive decoration*'. Perhaps they were aiming at 'shabby chic'. I wrote in my diary 'scruffy'.

Scruffy it may have been, but the beer was varied and the names even better. We tried the '*Holiday by Mistake*' (presumably a reference to the film Withnail & I[1]) and '*Atheists in Foxholes*' (i.e. there are no atheists in foxholes – the aphorism denoting that when the going gets tough people will believe in the existence of a deity). There

---

[1] British black comedy film about two unemployed actors in the 1960s.

were eight kegged beers and a couple of handpulls. This was going to take a bit of effort and commitment. I did my best finishing off with a 'Brown and Stout' at 8%.

Eight forty-five! Normally we'd have been on the road for an hour or more. We needed some fibre for breakfast. We had churritos – long piped doughnuts, rolled in sugar. Delicious but not the bowel scraping victuals that our bodies really required to keep us regular.

We had very much got into a routine of getting up early, splashing water on our face, counting items back into our rucksacks and then getting on the road before breakfast. Today we had nothing to do and it all felt a little strange, so we sauntered around the city. 'Saunter' comes from the French, 'Saint Terre' (Holy Land) and relates to those pilgrims walking that route. So, sauntering was a very pilgrimic activity.

The cathedral charged to enter. We'd seen countless gothic structures such as this so we skirted around to the gift shop to pick up a credential stamp and a post card.

We bumped into various acquaintances during the morning, all looking as lost as we were and, to a man and woman, we all said the place was lovely, but we were missing the walking. I was also missing the weight of my rucksack and felt far too light, walking with Neil Armstrong-like steps.

Our first choice of accommodation for León had not been the four star Holidaylodge Hiltoniott of last night but the splendid Hotel Hostal San Marcos. This parador (chain of Spanish historic, luxury hotels) was gothic with knobs on - and bells and whistles - and added extras. Our guidebook described it as 'plateresque' (in the manner of a silversmith). It was certainly impressive. Unfortunately, it was also closed for refurbishment. It was also the place the characters in '*The Way*' stayed at when they were treated by Martin Sheen for the night. In the film they all have their first taste of luxury for weeks and find that they preferred the camaraderie of being all together in the same room. I could relate to that.

A statue of a recumbent pilgrim faced the parador's entrance, head tilted to catch the warming rays of the sun, sat with his back protected by a stone cross. His hands crossed in mediative repose and a beard evidencing many weeks of inattention to matters bodily. Sore feet were now rid of their restricting sandals, those shoes bearing the imprints of many hundreds of kilometres, their bronzed leather tatty with wear. I adopted that same pose and was at one with my ancient travelling companion. I too understood his weariness and, at the same time, the serenity of the few moments of rest and peace that a simple sit down can give you. Lynne snapped us, side by side, and I knew that this would be the cover for this book. I only wish I'd taken my socks off. What a fashion blunder!

Every city has its quieter side, the backstreets where few tourists tread, even places where the local constabulary only travel in twos. Luckily, León didn't seem to have a rough quarter, at least we'd not found it. Meandering a few streets from the centre the street furniture had metamorphosised from marbled paving and regimented cast iron benches to cheap plastic chairs and tables, bearing the names of ice cream and beer sponsors. Our little café for lunch provided ineffectual paper plates that sagged under the moisture and grease of a dollop of paella. We carefully transferred our food to a vacant space and then dashed to pick up the ice cold beer left at the bar. For the next hour we watched life go by; couples kissing, friends hugging, children doing what children do – mainly running around and being told to "shush".

After a busy afternoon and before the locals venture out to start the whole process over again at around nine pm, there was a lull. Pilgrims used this as their safe time, a time when they could search out macaroni without being ridiculed or locked out of their accommodation for being late back.

I used this quiet time to seek out a local hop farmer that I had read about. Perhaps there was little Wi-Fi in the fields, perhaps he was very busy, perhaps he didn't want to be pestered by an English brewer, but my e-mails of the past few days had fallen on a deaf inbox. Having said that, this was not the straw munching 'get orf my land[1]' type individual I was seeking. This grower was producing a new wave of hops for young, bearded, pierced and backwards baseball cap wearing,

---

[1] A reference to unfriendly farmers.

hipster brewers; the sort who ran the Four Lions Brewery that I now found myself in. I asked about his whereabouts at the bar. He was in Madrid, doing something corporate, I was told.

Unsurprisingly, all the beers had lion related names: Wild Roar, Apex, Panthera Leo, Barbary, Untamed, Lion's Roast. I tried the lot. I would sleep well.

LEÓN – SARRIA

Week four.

Loaded with sugar and trans fats, churritos would raise my blood sugar levels, induce leptin and insulin resistance, elevate triglycerides and push cholesterol levels off the scale. They were heavenly. I could feel the glucose rush cascading though my lymphatic system from arm pits to groin. I was fighting fit to go. Unfortunately for me, if I carried on like this, I would be fit for nothing and fighting for breath.

It was a beautiful day, only spoilt by the knowledge that the UK was having an equally warm heat wave. If there is one thing that really makes a holiday, it's the thought of those back at home suffering.

Suburbs meant out of town shopping. After weeks of shopping like our grandparents during the Blitz, a couple of grams of mousetrap cheese here, a slice of cured spiced meat there, we had every modern convenience at our credit card disposal. We wouldn't need a trolley, not even a basket; if we couldn't carry it, it was not going to fit into our rucksacks. We bought travel wash and shower gel.

Our companions for the next few hours were white, unlogo'd lorries screaming past on the N-120. Each of these were numbered discretely with a white number (one to ten) in a small green square in the top left corner of each side. We wondered what these signified. Such was the extent of our excitement on this stretch of the route.

As we were walking along a main road, we decided to do as the lorry drivers do – stay at a truck stop; this one at the Spanish guitar player sounding name of Villadangos del Páramo.

TripAdvisor comments about these types of places were universally consistent - 'adequate' was the most used adjective. It was a motel. It was on a main road. It catered for truckers. What did people expect? The Ritz?

This place was more than adequate. True the vista from the window was nothing to write home about unless, of course, you were a truck spotter, and the electricity pylon buzzed a bit, but this was drowned out by the consistent rumble of vehicle tyres. It was, however, spotlessly clean, had a bar and a restaurant and was en route.

There was little to do, not that we had anything pressing in mind. We were in a motorway service area. We read our books, completed our diaries and watched the multi wheeled wagons go by. We invented 'lorry bingo'. Lynne and I both wrote down the numbers one to ten on a sheet of paper and took alternate white lorry numbers, crossing them off as we went. It got quite heated when we both needed a number seven.

"Come on. Get ready for dinner." nagged Lynne.

"I'm still waiting for number seven."

"Right, I'm going across on my own."

The bar was full of … lorry drivers. Obviously, pilgrims had read the reviews and preferred 'cheap' and 'macaroni' over 'adequate' and 'conveniently located on the busy N-120'.

A sign at the entrance of the bar advised us that the restaurant opened at eight thirty. Two hours. What to do, what to do? We did what the lorry drivers did. Drank beer.

A scraping of bar chairs alerted us to the opening of the restaurant as a dozen or so hungry truckers made their way to sit down. The dress code was checked shirts and hairy arms. We had neither. Tablecloths and starched napkins made it feel like an event. All that was lacking were candles and Villadangos the Spanish guitarist.

Two menus were passed to each of us. Both looked identical. We thought one may have been the pilgrims' menu the other the drivers'. We ordered from just one of them, lest we messed up their system.

The fish soup was very, very orange, served from a huge tureen, we watched others to see how much we should take. The others took lots, well they had much belly to fill. Next veal steak with a couple of potatoes. No vegetables. This no vegetable thing was getting a bit worrisome and I was beginning to think I may get scurvy by the end of the trip, but everyone else seemed to be coping with the food and perhaps the vitamin C came from the wine, which was a house 'Camino Frances' tinto. When we finished the tinto I hopefully asked if we could have a little more. The waiter, grabbed a bottle from another customer's table and plonked it on ours. No one batted an eyelid. Pudding was a bowl of custard with an added surprise. Deep in all that vanilla loveliness was hidden a soggy rich tea biscuit.

After the meal we were presented with a couple of shots of local lemon liqueur in frozen glasses, a nice touch, and with a couple of café solos the bill came to twelve euros each.

I was up extra early.

"What are you doing?" queried Lynne.

"Looking for a number seven."

Tonight's stop was Hospital de Órbigo and I was looking forward to some wholesome, local, artisan food. We passed the Philadelphia Cheese factory.

We had most of the day to kill. It had only been twelve kilometres and we had the advantage of riding on continuous pantechnicon slip stream allowing us to travel at speed trap velocities. Interesting fact: Pantechnicon was the name of a British storage company that used large vans to deliver and collect furniture.

History and literature today.

Luckily, the N-120 bypassed the town, the neat cobbled streets unsuitable for Michelin radials. Only those with two or four feet would pass into the centre. I thought I'd gone deaf without the roar of lorries.

The Rio Órbigo and its wide floodplain was traversed by a very long and ancient bridge. Not 'ancient' as in crumbling but as in 'been there for a long time'. Since the 13th century in fact. Today, the bridge is in very good repair and a tourist attraction, with its sable-coloured stone arches and cobbled surface.

At the river itself, a lone fisherman stood ankle deep in in thigh length gaiters (he wasn't taking any chances) hopefully catching our dinner for this evening. We looked down on him, waved and continued along the 200 metre long viaduct.

To our left was a billiard table flat flood plain with a military bearing, precise and ordered and with a skeletal viewing platform and central divide; all the accoutrements to a jousting tournament. Close your eyes and you could hear the clash of poles, the oohs and aaahs of the crowd as the knightly favour was held aloft by the victor, perhaps the detachable sleeve or handkerchief from his medieval lady. What she then blew her nose on is anyone's guess.

I had promised myself a day of history and literature and this came in the form of Suero de Quiñones in 1434. Don Suero fell in love with a Lady Leonor, who unfortunately did not fancy him back. To show his distress, the Don, every Thursday, both fasted and wore an iron collar to show that he was a 'prisoner of love'. Thinking that this, perhaps, didn't go far enough, he also challenged every knight in the vicinity to a joust known as the 'Honourable Passage'. Hundreds of knights took him up on his offer and Don Suero and nine of his mates (well, someone had to cover on Thursdays) fought man to man, horse to horse.

Don Suero said that when he had won 300 lances (competitions) he would take off the Thursday collar and would have served his time. The only problem was that he was relying on third-party help and support and, as we all know, if you're going to do a job, you're probably best doing it yourself. Firstly, many nobles wanting to cross the bridge weren't too keen on having a fight. These were allowed to throw down a glove and then ford the river below the bridge. Secondly, the Don's mates weren't as good as him and lost quite a few jousts.

The episode ended when the King got fed up with this charade and the locals were complaining that the annual cattle drive was being impeded. Therefore, a pools panel[1] decision was made that the sub 200 contests were sufficient to adjudge Don Suero the winner. The local judges ceremonially removed the collar and then sent him on pilgrimage to Santiago to keep him out of mischief and out of their hair.

So, why is this story of literary significance? Well, the story of this tournament, its romance and chivalry, inspired Cervantes to write *Don Quixote* a couple of centuries later. I had a copy with me and this was to be my literary companion for the next week or so.

The book, *The Ingenious Gentleman Don Quixote of La Mancha*, is oft quoted as being the first modern novel and revolves around a gentleman of fading years (golly, he's in his late forties) who has, in my parlance, gone a bit soft in the head or perhaps more politically

---

[1] A 'pools panel' was used to adjudicate the scores of football matches that had been postponed or abandoned for the 'Pools', a betting game forecasting the scores of British football matches.

correctly, had mental health issues. Having read any number of chivalric stories of romantic love, worthy deeds and derring-do Don Quixote starts living out his fantasies with his trusty squire, Sancho Panza.

Much of what I think I know about the book: his belief he is a knight-errant, being knighted by an inn-keeper, the book burning and tilting at windmills all appear in the first couple of chapters, perhaps foretelling of a difficult book which few get to the end of?

I was very much reminded of the relationship between Baldrick and Blackadder[1] in the first of the BBC TV series. Here, Baldrick is by far the more intelligent of the pair and despairs at Blackadder's ineptitude.

We sat at the balcony of the Hostal Don Suero, with its magnificent view of the bridge. The sun was shining and we drank freshly squeezed orange juice. Pilgrims waved at us and we waved back. We did a lot of waving.

Hospital de Órbigo had any number of quaint hostals but, for some reason, none of these came up on an Internet search and we had pre-booked another 'adequate' motel on the N-120. We went out in search of it, guided by a rumble of traffic, and bumped into Raymond and Barbara.

"We're staying in a lovely albergue." said Raymond. "Come in for a drink."

Raymond was right. It was lovely with its sturdy oak columns supporting a gallery of blue windowed rooms all overlooking a cobbled courtyard bedecked with pot plants and flowers. So much nicer than our CEPSA petrol station was going to be.

Disaster struck.

Packing for the Camino needed economy and ergonomy meaning everything in our rucksacks must be both

---

[1] Blackadder was a 1980s British sit-com starring Rowan Atkinson in the title role.

small, lightweight and (if possible) multi functional. The 'spork' was as good an example of this as anything. This was a plastic spoon, fork and knife all in one. It was great for picnics, cutting cheese, eating yoghurt etc. I sat on mine.

A large group of mourners were finishing up at a funeral and looked to be heading for the same restaurant as us for the wake.

"Lynne. Hurry up. We need to get in before them." I chivvied.

La Encomienda Restaurant was our choice of dining that evening as we had heard much about their trout soup, freshly caught from the Rio Órbigo. Our suspicion about the funeral party was correct and they were about to descend on the bar for ham sandwiches, or whatever the Spanish equivalent is.

We ordered the *sopa de trucha* not quite knowing what to expect. Imagine a savoury bread and butter pudding and then add pieces of chopped smoked trout to the mix. This was not a dish for the fainthearted. The trout was unfilleted and required a surgeon's skill and patience to remove the bones and skin. I'm not sure I particularly enjoyed it, but it was authentic.

This time 'adequate' did describe the previous night's accommodation. The receptionist yesterday had been sullen and uncommunicative to the point that she hadn't actually bothered to book us in and the morning staff were surprised to see us trot down the stairs in the morning for breakfast.

N-120 or scenic route? Decisions, decisions. Kilometres of sandy tracks were our choice and we set off with high hopes of a more serene path – Brierley would have been proud. Occasionally, we had to cross the main road, and I always had my eye open for a number seven lorry.

David's free pit stop, La Casa de Los Dioses, satisfied our physical needs. The proprietor had given up a life in business to serve pilgrims along the Way, asking nothing for the delicious pomegranate juices that we drank while relaxing in the sun. A hound of dubious parentage, rested lugubriously in the centre of a blanket, watching the world – at least the world of a pilgrim – go by.

Along the wide sandy path that was our route, we happened upon the tall poles of a hop farm, a verdant oasis amongst the dry sandy soil.

The Spanish have been growing hops for over a hundred years using irrigated water from the Órbigo river but these little rectangles of bines were new, to service the demands of the craft beer market. Up until a few years ago, the market would have been for the 'noble' hops that went into producing the light pilsner type beers. However, today, the root stock was very much that of the Americas with high alpha acid content (the stuff that makes beer bitter) and pungent citrussy and piney flavours and aromas so liked by modern beer aficionados.

A weather worn medieval cross, its base festooned with stones, marked our downward descent towards Astorga with its uniformly terracotta red roofs. A lone troubadour, who would not have been out of place in the Pampas of Argentina, serenaded us on our journey, his song; one of a repeated two lines about pilgrims walking into the town. It must have driven him nuts, although most of us tossed a few cents into his guitar case.

At the entrance to the town, we crossed a railway line with its Escheresque[1] bridge; an over-engineered construction if I'd ever seen one. Its purpose, to allow cyclists and pilgrims to cross a very  sleepy single branch line lest they fall prey to the slowly shunting stock pulling into the station. For some bizarre reason, Google Maps had labelled this as the *Peregrino Torture Tower*.

We passed the Roman remains of the city walls and military camp, the sewers, bath houses and sporadic mosaics. Again, we were reminded of the area's strategic military positioning. But the town was also at the end of the Vía de la Plata (the Silver Route) although there is no evidence of silver being traded along it. What it was, was a very ancient trade route and also an alternative route to Santiago, starting from Mérida in central, western Spain.

---

[1] Maurits Cornelis Escher, Dutch graphic artist 1898 – 1972. Famous for mathematically inspired and impossible drawings.

The main square was preparing for lunch. Proprietors were clattering aluminium tables and chairs into place and a few pilgrims were availing themselves of a late morning beer to wash away the dust of the route. We joined them, ensuring that we tried some of the local hops.

We were joined by a very knowledgeable German, Wilfred. The Camino pilgrims were a family and it was rare to sit alone and to be expected that any untaken seating would be soon occupied by fellow walkers. On the Camino, you are never alone. Unfortunately, we tended to attract the nutters. Wilfred had a well informed opinion on everything. However, his vast font of quirky facts soon grated and we

were looking for a polite excuse to leave. Luckily for us Raymond and Barbara walked into the town and we made our excuses to find a less erudite conversation with our South African friends.

We mooched around after lunch looking out for another of the town's exports, chocolate, as Astorga was its capital. However, we avoided visiting the Museum of Chocolate - far too tempting. Lynne did come across a rucksack that was even bigger than hers. She'd need more than a Rafael Nadal knee support to lift this!

After sufficient wandering, we located our bed and breakfast for the night, Descanso de Wendy, just a few decibel jarring metres away from the cathedral bell tower. We could have stayed at the four star spa hotel just down the road for the same price, but quirky was what we desired, especially after the roadside petrol stations of the previous evenings. Wendy did nothing by halves and her LSD-like colour schemes assailed the senses. This was a woman for whom 'subtle' didn't enter her vocabulary. Modern art of the more avant-garde movement adorned every free bit of wall space. We were never going to be able to get to sleep.

Our bodies were craving some vegetables. However, the local speciality was *cocido maragato*, a hotpot of eight meats with potato. This was a mixed grill on amphetamines. Shin of beef, ham hock, chicken, bacon, pancetta, pork trotters, pork rib, pigs' ears and finally the oink. And then there was a twist. The meal is served backwards. First served is the meat, then a dish of chickpeas and finally a vegetable soup.

"Mum can I have the vegetables please."

"No, not until you've eaten your meat."

I asked the proprietor why.

"Perhaps bandits would come and interrupt the meal." he said. A very good point.

Wendy's brave colour schemes also made it to the breakfast table with a dish of fresh oranges, strawberries and kiwis, pots of home made preserves, little cakes and some scrambled egg with mushrooms and ham. We loved Wendy.

Most of the villages in this part of Spain had changed little over the past thousand years. They were often cramped with narrow streets and passageways, originally designed for those on foot or perhaps a donkey pulled cart. They were not designed for the internal combustion engine. We sat outside a small café in Santa Catalina De Somoza and every five minutes the patrons picked up their chairs and tables and squeezed tightly against the wall to allow a Ford Transit to pass, in this case, a Jacotrans van carrying Lynne's rucksack. We wished it luck.

Time for another quirky lunch, the Meson Cowboy in El Ganzo. If you like eating in a garage, then this is the place for you. It's a rough and tumble establishment with mismatched chairs and tables and equally eclectic clientele. The star of the bar was Karma, a huge black and white bear of a dog who mugged pilgrims for food.

Give a pilgrim a wall and they will stack stones on it. Give them a fence and they will decorate it. Chain-link fences were the favourite as it was possible to intertwine sticks in the shape of a cross. Today's path took us into fenced scrubland, full of bits of twig. A herd of a few ginger brown cows watched bemusedly as we passed them, pulling off the crosses and eating them. If there was a cow heaven, they wouldn't be going there.

Choosing overnight accommodation was always hit and miss. The municipal albergues were guaranteed to be full of snorers and farters, anything really cheap was usually awful, but any place that looked after animals was always a safe bet. The proprietor at the hotel in Rabinal del Camino was feeding a clowder of village cats outside his front door. We booked in.

Time for the 'hunt the rucksack' game. Lynne and I had already split our clothes between the two rucksacks, so if one did go missing then we wouldn't be without something to wear. Lynne finally tracked down her bag at the municipal albergue and found Raymond sitting drinking a beer. He bought us one. We bought him one back and he bought us another. Then it was late afternoon. I had no idea where the time had gone – oh yes I did – drinking with Raymond. To soak up the beer we had a few ham croquetas which were described as being vegetarian.

As crazy as it sounds, we arranged to meet up with Raymond and Barbara for dinner. Supposedly, I had a long phone call with some friends in France after our meal. I'm afraid that I couldn't remember it.

Brierley had mentioned that the terrain was all up as we were heading for the highest part of the Camino. An early start was required. We had not ordered breakfast and were ready for the off at seven. The proprietor was waiting for us and asked if we wanted breakfast. We politely declined but he wasn't going to take 'no' for an answer.

"Sit. Sit." We sat at the bar and he made us a couple of milky coffees, then two huge tranches of cake appeared. Then, just as we were heading out the door he rushed after us to give us a container of freshly cracked walnuts for the journey. A lovely gesture.

'Majestic' was the word I used to describe the panorama that greeted us as we set off along the road. The mountains ahead of us reflected pink and orange in the early morning sun and it was going to be a lovely day. But we were heading up and we could see snow on the tops. However lovely it looked, it was also going to be cold.

There was an eerie silence today. The usual throng of pilgrims were absent. We knew why; our fellow walkers had been up especially early to get to the Cruz de Ferro (Iron Cross) at dawn.

"Try the fried eggs." A friendly couple advised us as we walked into Foncebadón. The village itself was nothing to write home about. A barn at its entrance had tumbled down. Pilgrims took each other's photos in front of it for their social media accounts – 'Our albergue for the night'.

The Hostel-Restaurant El Trasgu was the eggy destination and everybody was eating the house speciality. Two fried eggs on a piece of toasted baguette. That was it.

I have a list of my top ten meals ever. Very few of these are posh. I remember eating barbecued souvlaki in a wooden dining car on a tortuously slow Greek train in the Peloponnese and having freshly caught mackerel, pulled from the Bosporus and immediately swung from the end of the line into the hands of a street vendor, who gutted the still wriggling fish, serving it between two pappy slices of bread. These fried eggs would join them. The velvety, gooey yolk seeping pyroclasticly into the cratered bread. It was nursery food at its most basic.

Penny at the next table was worrying. She too had eggs. But hers were being rushed as she needed to get on. The reason? Penny had, on a whim, booked into a retreat along the route and five days later had emerged spiritually cleansed of all worldly cares – apart from the fact that her Iberian Airlines plane to the US ran to a fixed timetable and she would be five days late for it. I made all the right noises but inwardly didn't have much sympathy. Oh, and we still left before her as she told the same story to the next poor pilgrims cornered by her.

Every gram in the rucksack mattered. Each swing of the bag onto sore shoulders occasioned a groan. That's why I had a stone in mine. This pebble had come from a nearby beach at home and I had transported it 1,200 kilometres by public transport and 600 kilometres on my back.

The shrine at Cruz de Ferro rose up from a mountain of similar pebbles, a humilladero. What this totem symbolised is lost in the mists of time. The Romans may have worshiped Mercury here, it may represent the fact the medieval pilgrims often carried chunks of limestone to build chapels and churches along the way or it might just be a marker. I rummaged into my rucksack for my pebble.

Most stones had a message written on them. We had recently lost our pet Labrador of 14 years. Ozy would have loved this walk. I dedicated my stone to him. A special prayer accompanies the stone laying ceremony:

Lord, may this stone, a symbol of my efforts on the pilgrimage that I lay at the foot of the cross, weigh the balance in favour of my good deeds some day when the deeds of my life are judged. Let it be so.

I scrambled down towards Manjarin with zero gravity-like lightness, both in body and soul, now that my rucksack had delivered its cargo.

Manjarin wins top prize for the least inhabited village on the whole Camino – population: one. It also had accommodation. A quick search on the review sites had convinced us that, perhaps, this was not a place to tarry: '*Filthy and a health hazard*' and '*This is what the Camino of hundreds of years ago must have looked and felt like*' were representative opinions. Whilst I am not anti having an authentic experience, I was not sure that my Permethrin impregnated sleeping bag was quite up to the job.

Think Steptoe and Son's[1] slightly less tidy relative's scrap yard. Now you have some idea of the establishment. Run by Tómas, who

---

[1] British sitcom from the 1960s and 1970s about a father and son in the rag and bone business (collectors of rubbish for profit).

claims to be the last of the Knights Templars, the entrance is a mass of rainbow painted direction signs giving destinations and distances for far flung spots such as Budapest (2615 km) and Quito (9,700 km). it looked like Land's End on acid. Unsurprisingly, Tómas is the only resident of the hamlet, apart from the ubiquitous junkyard dogs.

Noticing that Santiago was 222 kilometres away, we thought that we had better not tarry and be on our way and, after buying a postcard for a euro, we continued, our retinas slowly recovering from the kaleidoscope experience that was Tómas' emporium.

The rolling green hills with Alpine horned cattle dotted around, together with the white peaked mountains in the distance gave the vista a Sound of Music[1] quality and I would not have been surprised to see a dirndl clad Maria yodelling across the valley.

Whilst many an establishment along the way could be guilty of hyperbole, we were keen to see what 'probably the best hostal on the Way' had to offer. The Albergue La Casa Del Peregrino promised a swimming pool and hydrotherapy centre; it had a lot to live up to.

Nestled in the rolling hills of the Bierzo region and with a mountainous backdrop the location was a very good start. Beds were ten euros but, for twice that amount, a double room was available. Snoring and sweaty bodies or peace, quiet and comfort? Decisions, decisions.

The room rivalled any boutique hotel in the UK. It was super modern with bold coloured walls and plenty of exposed stonework. The bathroom was awash with granite and marble and it even had trendy square taps that took me a while to work out how to turn on. Even the laundry facilities were luxurious and Lynne took the opportunity to wash everything she had whilst keeping a degree of modesty – just. One, usual gripe – no hanging space.

Despite the luxurious surroundings, the meal was definitely on the pilgrim spectrum. There was soup for starters and roast chicken quarter for mains. That was it. However, the fresh strawberries for dessert were good. Our routine of an espresso and a brandy after dinner

---

[1] American musical film and stage show, following the musical career and subsequent escape of a family of singers in Nazi Germany. Maria, the main character.

had become an addiction and given the volume of the brandy (bucket-sized) there was a possibility that we might overdose.

We found water in the minibar. This was good as I had as yet to discover how to get cold water out of the tap and, after the largest brandy in Spain, I needed to rehydrate. Penny (of the five-day retreat) joined us for breakfast. We were surprised to see her as she really did need to be much further on than she was. We finished our breakfast, leaving her to saunter through hers and, perhaps, find someone else to tell how behind she was.

Most of the Camino is well paved, but there are some quite rough and stony parts and this was one of them. We slowly picked a path over the uneven boulders and loose stone, often skidding ten or so centimetres. The greatest fear for most pilgrims is an ankle sprain. Actually, the greatest fear is getting to an overnight stop to find that there's no bar. We were therefore careful on all fronts.

We bumped into Raymond and Barbara again. Raymond was sporting an eye patch giving him a suave buccaneer look. He'd been fine the day before. Perhaps that's why we hadn't seen him the previous evening. I never did get to the bottom of why he had it on.

We were looking forward to Ponferrada (Latin, pons ferrata - iron bridge) for two reasons: firstly, it was the capital of the El Bierzo region with a reputation for good wine and secondly, it had a couple of craft beer bars. All we now had to worry about was that ankle.

Raymond went off to get his pitch for the night whilst we had the luxury of having pre-booked our hotel and so could explore the centre of the old town. It didn't take long.

At the top of the Plaza Ayuntamiento was Cerveceros del Bierzo, a micropub specialising in local brews. Looking at my diary later, I had written descriptions such as 'pokey' and 'robust'. Ideal for a lunchtime snifter.

Our hotel that night was of the modern budget box variety where staff are scarce and if you haven't a mobile phone to check in with, then you're stuffed. It was also a bit out of town. Luckily, we did have a phone with our booking on it and thus were able to access our room. I say 'room', the Google dictionary definition stated: '*space that can be occupied or where something can be done'*. Yes, we could occupy it, but getting something done in it was going to be difficult. It had a bed but the floorspace between that and the wall needed a feeler gauge to measure it. I could just about get round the bed, but only if I wasn't wearing my socks. Luckily, I'd had robust and pokey beers at lunchtime so it wasn't a problem as I wasn't going to move for a good few hours.

Call me a traditionalist, but I do like to drink my beer out of a glass. The Chelsea Bar was a brief respite from all things Spanish. It was very 1960s London with film posters depicting a young Michael Caine and plenty of miniskirts. The only problem was that they were serving beer in jam jars. I think they thought it was trendy, or perhaps they thought that that's all we had to drink out of in sixties' London.

As we were in a town we took advantage of having a choice of restaurants and plumped for a pizzeria and a bottle of the local Bierzo wine, appropriately named 'Pilgrim'. All we had to do now was to locate our dolls' house sized hotel room again, find the app to open the door, squeeze into the room – all this after popping back to the lunchtime micropub venue for a pokey and robust nightcap.

The breakfast room of the hotel had been stocked by invisible fairies and we were able to have a cup of coffee and a croissant before setting off for the day, still having seen no one. I consulted the guide. The map scaling in our Brierley appeared to have changed. The distance on the page looked similar to the previous days but the distance was getting on for 25 kilometres which was, in my opinion, a bit of an ask.

Our route out of town took us past a modern sculpture in the middle of a roundabout. Curiosity got the better of me and I braved the traffic to have a look. Whilst we blood donors in the UK get a cup of tea and a dibby biscuit, those in Spain get a monument to them and the needle-like monument was, in fact, a bronze drop of blood. From here we passed through a landscape of post-industrial slag heaps from the, now defunct, coal industry. The Museum of Energy reaffirmed that this was an important part of the town's past.

The drab post war communist-style architecture continued into the suburbs. A block of flats, probably built to house the coal workers, had that late night horror film look to it. Out of the corner of my eye I was sure I caught glimpses of deranged mental patients screaming silently from barred windows.

We passed swiftly through and on reaching a lone church were enchanted by the murals around the door depicting the passing of the agricultural year. November was particularly graphic with a pig being hit neatly on the head with an axe.

After the city and its tenement blocks for the workers, the countryside villages were neatly kept and obviously a commuter belt for the town. At Camponaraya, a village fiesta was in its infancy with bleary eyed locals decorating the streets with bunting and worthy-looking volunteers deciding where to place barriers with Chuckle Brothers'[1] precision. A Galician bagpipe band rehearsed a cat-eviscerating melody outside the 'Traditional Music School', depicted by a Banksy-esque[2] mural. I was pretty sure that the neighbours must have received a reduction in their local taxes at this end of town.

Again, this was wine country with a mixture of old and gnarled vines, like rheumatic fingers emerging from the earth and then brand new plants in regimented rows, ready for mechanical picking.

In keeping with the money that this area attracted, we stopped at an artisan farm shop and café. Whilst we never actually found the entrance to the café itself, the shop was crammed full of local produce and whilst Lynne was using the toilet, I picked up a bar of hand made chocolate as a birthday present for her. Perfect; light, easily concealable and I could help her eat it.

---

[1] An English comedy/slapstick double act. One of their most famous sketches being the moving of furniture/a ladder/plate of glass in an uncoordinated fashion.

[2] Anonymous English street artist.

Further down the road was a café that did actually have an entrance and we accompanied our coffee with highlights from the previous night's Eurovision Song Contest. A young woman lurched toward us, obviously already in fiesta mode, explaining that Israel had won the contest and that by an incredible coincidence she too was Israeli. She and her companions had been celebrating all night. It showed. Spain had come fourth with a Jason and Kylie-like[1] duet and the UK had come third from last after Dr AC Activism, an urban guerrilla and self-publicist had stormed the stage and grabbed the mike. The Israeli young woman told us this was very unfair. We taught her that the correct expression was "We woz robbed" which she practiced a few times with drunken concentration before re-joining her equally happy friends to fiesta some more.

Back to the vines and a tragedy. A small group of us snaked down a steep path when a young French woman took a nasty tumble right in front of us. Pilgrims far and wide rushed to her assistance. Great, I thought, an opportunity to use the first aid kit that had been contributing 250 grams of dead weight to my pack.

After consultation between the pilgrims in a mixture of English, Spanish and French it was obvious that nothing was broken, well at least there were no bits of bone sticking out, and we cobbled together a splint made from a crepe bandage, a sheet of newspaper and, I was particularly proud of this, a strip of duct tape that I had brought with me. There is nothing that cannot be repaired with duct tape (or a hammer).

After all this Good Samaritaning, I had worked up a thirst and appetite and luckily, we were just a stone's throw from Villafranca del Bierzo, our overnight stop. Lunchtime beer, chorizo and chips sorted me out. Lynne had something she thought might be fish.

The town promised a local delicacy, 'Botillo del Bierzo' and in the evening we went in search of it. The menu described it as *giant beans with pork's nose* – sell it to me. Well, in for a penny, in for a pound. I sat drinking my beer and, with my computer tablet, looked up what I was just about to eat. *www.meatsandsausages.com* was very helpful,

---

[1] Jason Donovan and Kylie Minogue are Australian actors and singers, first appearing in the soap opera, *Neighbours*.

'smoked sausage which is stuffed into a pig's cap which is the beginning of the large intestine and may also include: tongue, jowls, shoulder and spine.' The waiter helpfully showed me how to cut it open and by the look on his face he was obviously glad it was me eating it rather than him. Lynne had rabbit with Canarian potatoes. Lynne had chosen more wisely I thought. Pudding was vanilla custard with hidden rich tea biscuit – always a lovely surprise.

The friendly owner, as some sort of consolation prize, gave us a complimentary liqueur to take away the taste of the botillo. It was very welcome.

It may have been the elevation or perhaps we were in some sort of Einsteinian space time continuum but distance was now very fluid. The route took us through half a dozen small villages as we criss-crossed the Rio Valcarce. Each of these little hamlets had attempted to guess the distance to Santiago and, even though they were only a kilometre apart, the signposts varied wildly with us gaining and losing tens of kilometres as we passed through them.

Suddenly a stick appeared in front of me. A man was brandishing a stick and gesturing that I should take it. I'm not much of a stick man myself and, as far as I can see, walking poles have one purpose and one purpose only, and that is the inconvenience of forgetting them, resulting in additional miles retracing steps to retrieve the said stick from some bar. I made to give the man a small donativo, but he waved me away, saying it was a gift.

On reaching Vega de Valcarce, our stop for the day, our first priority was to find some accommodation. Actually, that was a lie. My first priority was to have a beer, and then find some accommodation.

The accommodation we found was a brand new pension with a very keen and attentive proprietor who relished stamping our credentials. No doubt, in a few months' time and after hundreds of dirty and bedraggled pilgrims, the enthusiasm would wear off.

The local panaderia (bread shop) had been recommended to us for dinner and we had the entrecôte steak, which was probably veal. At the next table a German couple; great anglophiles. I complimented the man on his English and he told me that his father had married in Taunton, just down the road from where we live in Somerset. We swapped telephone numbers and addresses. We would be seeing a lot more of Wolfgang and Elke.

Our host was as enthusiastic this morning as the previous day and gave us cake and pancakes for breakfast. As we left, we were presented with a small gift; a couple of decorated and 'branded' clothes pegs providing the pension's address. This was a lovely gesture and very well thought out. We pilgrims often needed to pin or peg items of clothing to our rucksacks, usually socks, and this would really come in handy. If the owner ever had to stop running a B and B, then she should consider a career in marketing.

Horizontally, the day was going to be short; vertically it was not, with 700 metres of climb ahead of us. We were in the mountains on our way to O Cebreiro.

Given the steep ascent, the locals had organised alternative transport in the form of a team of horses available for hire at Herrerías. 'Team' would suggest something organised. These horses were of the petulant teenager type who were not going to get out of their straw pit until oats had been produced and it was past midday.

We hadn't planned to hitch a lift and I thought it was a bit of a cheat. I wouldn't be surprised if you got some of your stamps taken away from your credential. So, we strode onwards and upwards soon entering into a wide landscape of purple heather blanketed hillsides. Horses and their unprincipled pilgrims passed us occasionally and a feeling of smugness came upon me. I was a real pilgrim, one who walked every step of the way, with a full rucksack.

A self-professed gastrobar welcomed us in for a café con leche en route. It didn't seem very 'gastro' unless the owner coughing into my coffee was part of the up-market service. However, the views were stunning. It was also playing *Hotel California*, the anthem of the Camino.

On a warm Galician byway
Sun bleaching our hair
One sniff of the albergue
Of sweaty socks in the air...

We were due a department change, crossing out of Castilla y Leon and into Galicia – 'Octopus Country'. The Romans called it 'the end of the earth'. We would find out if it really was in a week or so's time.

The fact that O'Cebreiro is situated on top of a high ridge, surrounded by mountains means that it attracts both pilgrims and day trippers and therefore there was plenty of accommodation, shops and restaurants. We were going to be spoilt for choice. Having said that, the first hostal had a large tan and white dog languishing in the entranceway and, as he seemed friendly enough, and using our pet friendly criteria for choosing places to stay, we decided this would be our stop for the night.

We explored the shops, bought postcards and examined the tat. A lapel badge caught my attention, 'Ibuprofen – the drug of the Camino'. I stealthily bought it for Lynne's birthday. Egg, bacon and chips for lunch with wine poured at the table directly from a wine box – classy.

A visit to the Romanesque church of Santa María killed half an hour. It dated back to the ninth century and it was here that Elías Valiña Sampedro was buried. This was the Spanish pastor who promoted the modern Camino as we know it today and had the idea of marking the route with the yellow arrow. Out he would go every day in his beaten up Citroën GS retracing the original route. Yellow was his colour of preference as it 1) was easy to see, 2) often used in way marking and 3) was the only paint he had in the back of his shed. On one occasion, he was stopped by the French Civil Guard whilst he was painting his arrows. On being asked what he was doing, Sampedro said "Preparing for the invasion of France". He was promptly arrested. No sense of humour those French.

We counted six restaurants in the town, all with identical menus. Now, I don't want to be picky, but with so many eating establishments I would have thought that one could have done things differently; perhaps a pizzeria or something a bit more up market? I had the potato and cabbage soup, chicken and chips and flan for dessert. The man next to me had the same, but in a different order. The table of six next to him, never had any of their crockery removed, so it just piled up. And, guess what? We had wine box wine poured at the table - it was tradition.

My theory was that the proprietors and the staff, living in this remote corner of the country, had no concept of what the modern pilgrim expected and how things had moved on in the outside world. Or, perhaps, this is exactly what the average pilgrim wanted. Whatever, the town could really have done with a bit of a kick up the backside.

However many gripes I had with the food or the service, the views more than made up for any little niggles and we were treated to *the* most gorgeous sunset; mountains and clouds bathed in the deep orange furnace of the setting sun. I was getting quite poetical and half an hour went by with us standing in silence as the sky darkened and night enveloped us.

The roseate glow of a perfect sunrise peeked around the shutters, revealed in all its glory as we threw open the windows to greet the day; but golly, it was a bit nippy.

A hopelessly inefficient café opposite was doing a roaring trade in mixing up orders and disappointing customers. We managed to get a coffee, someone else's we thought, and then, when we were unable to catch anyone's attention to pay, guessed at the cost, leaving the coins on the counter. All of us were donning fleeces.

Being so high, there was only one way to go – down. Down was good and as we descended, the temperature increased and we had soon divested ourselves of coats and jumpers. Perhaps, that's why I had a bit of a downer on O'Cebreiro. I was just a bit chilly.

If you had asked me what I had expected of the walk, this would have been it. Lush rolling pastureland, distant snow-capped mountains, quaint falling down villages and complete silence. Well, mainly silence; a Portuguese couple kept leap-frogging us, invading my space and chattering incessantly. What could they possibly have to say to each other? Lynne and I had run out of conversation by Day Two.

Given that my first impression of the Galicians was that they were a bit slapdash and disorganised, they had a precision for distances and each of the Camino distance markers gave the kilometres to Santiago to three decimal places. The one we were looking at stated 156.367km to Santiago. The only problem was that they are all ludicrously inaccurate, inconsistent and pointless.

Pilgrims queued at the Monumento do Peregrino (Alto San Roque)  whilst other pilgrims offered to take pictures for them. If you see anyone who does not have this picture in their portfolio, then you know that they are one of the Sarria pilgrims, who will be discussed later in this book.

The pilgrim monument wasn't the only touchy feely experience of the day. At the entrance to Triacastela was an eight hundred year old chestnut tree, rubbed smooth by the thousands of hands that had stroked it for luck. To think that this would have been a sapling in the twelve hundreds, a hundred or so years after Picaud's Codex Calixtinus and perhaps in the heyday of the twelfth and thirteenth centuries when a quarter of a million pilgrims or so would have walked the Way. I must remember to wash my hands.

There were no castles at the town of the three castles. The thermometer on my watch read 49°C in the direct sunlight. Beer was five degrees, so it made perfect sense to set one off against the other. My physics may not have been quite perfect so I had another in the spirit of scientific experimentation.

I had been e-mailing a possible hostal for this evening and when I had the opportunity to retrieve my e-mails, now on my second pint, I found that I had received a reply to my awful Spanish telling me a room had been reserved. The owner was very welcoming, praising me for my near perfect Spanish (liar) and we settled down for a short kip.

A short kip is exactly what we got as a group of four very excitable Canadian women swarmed into the hostal, each with a pantechnicon of luggage which they trundled on little plastic wheels up and down the wooden corridor floors. Then they all took very long hot showers. I had very short cold shower as a consequence.

The town boasted a number of bars, but with the hot sun, all the outside tables had been taken by beer swilling pilgrims. Others were having an early dinner. What did they do for the rest of the evening?

With time to kill before the six o'clock swill cleared, we meandered around the village and along the Rio Oribio. An information board informed us that there were bears in residence in the locale. I'd have to keep an eye open for them.

By now the restaurants were starting to declutter themselves of rucksacks and walking paraphernalia and we made our way back to the Parrillada Xacobeo, our lunchtime haunt. The clean and well coiffured Canadians were now in residence, even buzzier than before, fuelled with cheap wine. We introduced ourselves and, yes, we were correct, they were novices with their first day's walking tomorrow. I was able to impart the font of my knowledge to them, including the fact that they should beware of the bears; well, being Canadians, they would know what to do.

Our table occupied part of the courtyard and with the green artificial grass beneath our feet and the red gingham tablecloth we felt very continental. Starter was a large plate of paella and with it came a bottle of very cheap red, its label photocopied and stuck on with Pritt[1]. It wasn't very good, and I'm being polite here, so we generously donated it to the Canadians and ordered a single vineyard, Ribera del Duero 2014 Crianza.

Mains were fresh river trout and hake, reminding us that we were near the sea in this corner of the country. O'Cebreiro cheese for dessert, with milk from cows grazed on the lush pasture of the mountains that we had just passed through, its tartness offset by local honey and membrillo (quince) jam. The wine did it proud.

The Canadians, were discussing a shower rota for the morning. Whatever they did, they would be very clean doing it. I made a note to myself to have my wash before they got up.

Whilst it had been a very warm evening, a coolness from the surrounding mountains began to seep into the village and we moved inside for coffee and something to keep the chill away. We pondered

---

[1] World's first glue stick.

127

our bill over drinks and decided that it probably wasn't ours (far too low) and paid what we thought it should have been. The owners were delighted. The poor pilgrim who received our bill was probably not so happy.

The water guzzling Canadians were up at 6.00am, stock car racing their Samsonite suitcases up and down the corridors again. I very much doubted that any of them would be treading their knickers with shower gel during their evening ablutions and may even have had a quick change of clothing and a shower at midday.

PILGRIM, DO NOT ALLOW DOGS TO FOLLOW YOU! MOST OF THEM HAVE HOME AND BECOME HOMELESS FOREVER WHEN LOST!

They were up early. We were up earlier and after a quick café con leche we were on our way. Already lazy dogs were littering the path in the early morning heat. Not only were we to be on the look out for the ursine fauna, the canines were even more prevalent. Signs constantly reminded us not to befriend them lest they got lost.

Chapels abound during the next part of the trip, many in poor states of repair, uncared for, their skeletal remains all that was left of their former glory. Pilgrims would have perhaps stopped at each of these to offer up prayers but today, even those in reasonably good shape appeared to be given a cursory glance by pilgrims before they continued along their way.

Our Israeli song contest acquaintance was on the road today, somewhat more sober than when we had last met her, but no less enthusiastic. Perhaps it was drugs?

A sign promised a '*unique stop*' and '*powerful art*' 350 metres off piste so we headed towards it. The little hippy enclave served breakfast of the bowel cleansing variety and I bought some fresh dates to give the old innards a thorough workout. The owner explained to me that the shell attached to my rucksack was a symbol of completing the Camino and I should only pick one up in Santiago. I was going to explain that this wasn't just any shell but a Marks and Spencer shell[1], but I feared the irony would have been lost on her. My diary entry for the day clearly states she was talking rubbish.

We were now in Sarria, the start of the Camino for the vast majority of pilgrims who walk the route and want to get a Compostela. This had both advantages and disadvantages. On the plus side, it had loads of accommodation and we happened upon a brand new hostal on the outskirts of the main town. They had rooms and it looked like we were going to have a very comfortable stay there.

With our rucksacks stowed safely, we headed into the bustling town centre. After a week of small hamlets and villages, being in a busy and noisy environment was claustrophobic. And with busy and noisy came rip off establishments and rude staff. This was the negative side.

The Mesón o Tapas had come up on our radar and we ordered a couple of beers. It was a lovely spot, sitting outside in the sun and watching the world and crippled pilgrims walk by. The waiter came up to us three times to ask whether we wanted anything to eat. On the fourth time, and in order to shut him up, we ordered a small plate of chorizo and chips between us. "You must be very hungry" said the sarcastic waiter as he walked away.

The food was actually very nice; well, as nice as sausage and chips can be and we decided to order a plate of local cheese.

"Do you have any local red to accompany the cheese" asked I.

"Yes" said he, bringing back a wine box of Europlonk. However, the lunch ended on a high note when the bill arrived and half the items had been missed off. Result.

Back to base and the opportunity to use the state of the art washing facilities. This could be our last opportunity to properly wash our stuff and so everything went in, which was going to mean a few underwear clad dashes from the bedroom to the laundry room.

Architects! Imagine you are designing a hotel room. Modern styling means a wet room, perhaps one with one of those monsoon shower heads and then, why not put the toilet paper holder under the

---

[1] Marks and Spencer's advertising promotes its food as 'Not just any food, but Marks and Spencer food'.

shower? There should be a law; all architects should be made to live in the rooms and buildings they design for 24 hours.

How much different our pre-dinner drinks were from the lunchtime establishment. Convivial surroundings at the riverside bar, friendly serving staff, free tapas (lovely fish pasties, cheese and ham rolls and home-made crisps) and a nice range of beers - I had the tostada, a brown ale made with roasted malt.

The plan was to visit the pulperia opposite the bar for some octopus, but by the time we had finished our beer, it had closed. I think we had stumbled on yet another bank holiday; there had been a lot while we were out there. Plan B was to look for another restaurant. A buzzing bar took our fancy and we found a counter table and sat on the high chairs surveying the other diners.

We spotted the very clean and immaculately attired Canadians and caught up with their news, told with Labrador-like exuberance. An Irish couple sat at the next table and they had a concern. This was the very start of their journey and they were trying to explain to the non-Irish speaking waiter that they didn't want their red wine to be chilled. We got into conversation and passed on our pilgrim menu tip, which was that the wine would be undrinkable warm and they would be better off ordering water with the meal and getting a better bottle off the menu.

And so back to our room and the still wet floor and soggy toilet paper.

SARRIA - SANTIAGO DE COMPOSTELA

Almost immediately, we spotted a difference in the pilgrims walking the path. Mostly they were clean. They also didn't limp as much. Universally they were like excitable puppies straining at the leash, keen to get going. One Irishman we spotted had a crease in his walking trousers. Perhaps he had a Corby trouser press[1] in his rucksack – it was big enough. Collectively they were known as the 'plastic pilgrims' by those who had already walked 700 or so kilometres. Sometimes they were called nastier things.

From this point on, all pilgrims needed two stamps per day in their credential. This is not a problem as there are plenty of places to get a stamp. As for why this is necessary – this was anyone's guess.

We already had some idea of what this part of the route looked like as we had watched a BBC reality programme, *'Pilgrimage: The Road to Santiago'*, where seven celebrities spent a couple of weeks on the path. We were often asked if we had seen the programme and universally we disliked one of the participants, one Kate Bottley, a vicar and professional Northerner[2] who complained throughout the whole trip. However, the scenery in the programme was fantastic and it probably inspired many people to walk the path.

The route out of town hugged the railway line, derelict we thought, until a train dieselled past, honking its air horns, pilgrims waving, driver possibly wishing he could veer off the track and mow a few of them down. Perhaps not.

We were definitely in green Spain and the path meandered around fields of lush pasture. Combine harvesters were cutting the grass and resident white storks surveyed the aftermath, no doubt in search of evicted rodents and lizards. Drying houses for corn were evident in most every field and farmyard. These were narrow sheds, raised off the ground on mushroom shaped stones (no doubt to deter rats) with

---

[1] A ubiquitous but largely unused piece of hotel equipment invented by RAF veteran Peter Corby. The butt of many a sit-com joke.

[2] A professional Northerner is a derogatory expression about a person extolling the benefits of living in the north of England (often Yorkshire). The term mocks class, living standards and accent.

air-bricks or wooden slatted sides. The Galicians call them 'horreos' and they were landmarks. Each had similar architecture, a pointed obelisk at one end and a cross at the other.

Galicia also had another unique landmark; the Miróesque[1] cartoon pilgrim appearing in signage along the way. This Mickey Mouseish pilgrim would accompany us for the next 100 kilometres.

At Mecadoiro, yet another one horse, or in our case, one bar, town we stopped for a beer, a birthday beer for Lynne. I retrieved the now crushed and semi-melted bar of chocolate that I had purchased a few days before. I'm not sure she was that impressed with the ibuprofen badge either.

ABBA's[2] Greatest Hits blared out. Two Argentinians in identical yellow fluorescent jackets, trailing converted shopping trollies, entertained by singing along with amplified Bjorn and Benny. They were the *Walking Queens*.

The way markers were counting down, in thousandths of a kilometre, towards the 100 km point. This is the minimum distance that pilgrims need to walk in order to get their certificate of completion, the Compostela. No stamps, no certificate. It doesn't matter how far you've walked. Those were the rules.

Many of the waymarks now had the words '*Melted Rubber Humans*' graffitied on to them. I later found out that these were an experimental electronica band hailing from Glasgow. Other mind boggling graffiti included a few days of '*Wild Sheep*' for no apparent reason and one signpost, just after leaving Sarria, which said '*Sarria Pilgrims F*** Off*'.

Another photo opportunity, the 100km way marker. Those waiting took photos of those posing. This was insurance just in case the

---

[1] Joan Miró, surrealist Spanish painter.
[2] Swedish pop band. Bjorn and Benny were the two male singers and musicians in the group. *Dancing Queen* was one of their most successful hits.

officials at Santiago wanted additional proof that we'd walked the route, as if our broken bodies were not enough.

The shops became a little more sophisticated along this latter stretch of the path and I was taken with the shell shop with its hand painted designs and, as I had now passed on the chocolate to Lynne, I could afford the extra weight of a shell. Mine said *'He who thinks little errs much'*. How true.

It was the Argentinians who took our photo. ABBA had been replaced by *'Nessun dorma'* from *Turandot*, sung with gusto. None would sleep through that.

I decided that, as my stick was now giving me a blister on the palm of my hand and the risk of bears had abated, I would donate it to a more worthy pilgrim and wrote a note wishing them good luck and left it on the side of the road. It wasn't very long afterwards that I saw it again being carried by an American woman. I was very pleased it had gone to a good home.

We descended steeply into Portomarín, catching glimpses of it to our right, across the wide Miño River. Our first priority was to find some accommodation. We stopped at the first bar and asked. No room at the inn. We bumped into a friendly face who said he had tried all the smaller hostals and there was nothing doing. He said the best he could find was a dormitory with 27 others. Snoresville here we come.

The next bar kindly did some ringing around for us and said that there was nothing available below 70 euros (which wasn't going to be a problem) but he had a suspicion that a residential apartment block just a stone's throw away from the centre would have some rooms – he was right and they found us a reasonably priced room. Next, hunt the rucksack.

The first port of call was the municipal albergue, only to find that this would not allow bags to be delivered. Why this was so was a mystery, every other albergue had opted for this system and, given that most pilgrims do not know where they will be resting that night, it made sense. Not only did they not take bags, they were particularly unhelpful in giving any clues as to where the bags may have been taken.

Sherlock Holmes time again. We needed to put ourselves in the head of a Spanish delivery driver. We went for a beer. Wolfgang and Elke joined us. They insisted we had a birthday drink with them and gave Lynne a small medallion they had bought for her birthday. A lovely touch. But we couldn't sit drinking beer all afternoon, we had a bag to find.

Actually, it wasn't that large a town and the number of possibilities were limited so it wasn't long before a very helpful hostal pointed to a large pile of bags where Lynne's was soon located.

We returned to the helpful bar that had given us the heads up on our accommodation and soaked up the last rays of the sun. Peter from Alabama joined us.

Peter had recently lost his wife and was walking the path alone. We discussed the merits and demerits of various types of accommodation and decided that having one's own room still beat the more authentic experience of sleeping with dozens of others in a sweaty and snore filled dormitory. We also asked why Peter didn't have an Alabama accent. The answer, "I'm from Ireland".

When in Galicia there is no option but to eat octopus at some stage and at the Restaurante Perez the boiled octopus with sea salt, paprika and plain boiled potatoes was as authentic as it got. It seemed a bit of a shame to eat these creatures, with their huge brains and blue blood. However, they were delicious.

Breakfast was Tarta de Santiago, a ground almond cake with a hint of citrus peel and dusted with icing sugar with the cross of Saint James on the top. Our waitress didn't smile.

Perhaps the road out of town was particularly dangerous, bandits hiding behind every hedge, but we acquired personal bodyguards in the form of three huge shepherd dogs of indeterminate breed who took it upon themselves to guide our small group of pilgrims along the path.

134

It really did seem that they were doing some sort of job and after ten minutes or so, they barked us a friendly goodbye and retraced their steps to bring another group safely along the Way.

A short detour at Castromaior enabled us to visit some very well-preserved Roman remains at a hill fort. The site was eerily quiet as most pilgrims chose not to deviate from the path and we sat in solitude and silence with magnificent views of the surrounding green and luscious countryside.

Back on the official route we got into steps with the usual suspects all known by some personal nickname: Stuart the Bus Pilgrim (only walked to bus stops), The Mad Israeli Song Contest Woman (she said she had missed us the previous day), the Bearded Belgian and the Four French.

Given the numbers now walking along the route, the various establishments had to up their game a bit in order to process increasing volumes of traffic and the pilgrim motorway service area style café was ultra efficient in getting food and drinks into their customers.

Harry and Meghan[1] were getting married. Most pilgrims were not interested. We were not particularly interested. The Spanish loved it.

Given the difficulty finding accommodation we had decided to book the next two nights in advance and tonight's was a country resort, a log cabin affair. If we thought we were going to have a peaceful time, then we were sadly mistaken and a confirmation party meant that the place was swarming with children, doing what children do – mainly running around screaming.

Ignoring the children breaking bones when falling off the bouncy castle, we sat on the veranda of the bar, sipping a beer. If this was life,

---

[1] Prince Harry and Meghan Markle.

bring it on. We watched pilgrims walk on by, no doubt to their crowded albergues. Stuart the Bus waved. Irish Evelyn and Damien saw us and joined us (they were the cold red wine complainers from Sarria) and we soon learnt that we were definitely in one of the lower divisions in the drinking league as they swiftly demolished three large beers with us.

Had it just been the beers, then we would have been fine, but then came the sangria, well iced and tasting like pop. We drank it like pop too. I know this as I had subtly changed from using the English language in my diary to some form of cruciform interspersed with various symbols ❤ ♪ ☺.

As the Irish left us to find more seasoned drinkers, we headed, carefully, off to dinner and met with Wolfgang and Elke, who naively, invited us to join them for food and wine. This was never going to end well and the conversation veered on to religion, Nietzsche and Kant. Given that I have very little knowledge of German philosophers and am a non-believer, it must have been an enlightening evening for my table companions. And then we had a brandy.

Still alive. Obviously, that which does not kill us makes us stronger (Nietzsche). See, I did know something about German philosophers.

Abusing the hotel's generosity on the buffet front, we stole enough food for lunch. The French Four were at the next table and they complained that Spanish cutlery was rarely sharp (I can't say I had noticed) and that the knives they had been given were 'aussi émoussé que le genou d'une religieuse' ('as blunt as a nun's knee'). A lovely expression.

In the spirit of continuing to comment on those who were only walking from Sarria, a group of Spanish women came to the breakfast room in perfectly laundered walking trousers and brilliantly white linen shirts. These would obviously not be breaking into a sweat or ruining the fine cut of their shirts by carrying a rucksack.

Mid morning coffee was taken in some entrepreneurial soul's front garden, specialising in instant Nescafé, where we passed the time with Frank and his daughter Katy from California (exuberantly religious), a French lawyer and Irish engineer. It still astounded me that people were so open, so quick with names, occupations and the state of one's feet being provided without any prompting. Today's conversation was about Brexit. The French thought we were mad (the British leaving Europe, not us personally). The Irish thought we were mad (us personally). We, the French and the Irish thought the Californians were mad.

With two stamps needed a day, there was no shortage of places to dig out our passports and in a piece of waste ground on the way to Melide a couple were doing a thriving business making wax seals for the credential. This involved choosing the appropriate brass stamp (I chose a fleur de lis) with two little feet attached to a green ribbon. As I blew on the wax to cool it, it occurred to me that, as it was my intention to have my credential framed on my return to Blighty[1], sticking three dimensional things into my passport would test the framer's skill.

Melide was a modern town with characterless, grey, modernistic square buildings abutting busy roads. Pilgrims thronged and we saw familiar faces a plenty and sat with the Californians who were taking this pilgrimage thing far too seriously, studiously regarding the cathedral of Santiago's service times, like a bus timetable, to ensure their arrival coincided with the right mass.

Melide was also Octopus Central. After beers, we went in search of a light lunch and found the perfect spot, a garden patio in a pulperia, the Casa Alongos, which was also the name of their signature dish, a 100% octopus burger, served between artisan bread and a grilled courgette salad with a crisp, dry white wine. After weeks of mediocre and sometimes very poor service, this restaurant was an oasis of impeccable attentiveness with the friendly owner taking time to chat with us, helping us choose a wine and genuinely interested in knowing where we came from.

You need never be lonely on the Camino and our early evening drinks were taken on the pavement of the busy road through the town with various acquaintances we had met over the last few days. However, with the prospect of a pilgrim menu being ordered en masse

---

[1] English slang term for Great Britain.

137

we made our very polite excuses and headed back to our hostal which promised 'meat from the grill'. Don't get me wrong, there is nothing better than eating and drinking with new friends, it was just that yet another dreary macaroni in red sauce had lost its appeal.

'Carnage in the abattoir' was the best description of the steak and rack of pork ribs, unceremoniously thrown into the roaring furnace that was the horno. The resulting charred and extremely messy dish emerging from the inferno was sublime. How glad we were that we had resisted the pasta and Euro-plonk wine that our companions were no doubt tucking into in their ten euro joint.

My diary said we laid in to 7.00am. A custard croissant and coffee for breakfast whilst reading about the previous day's royal wedding, which occupied the front pages of *all* the national newspapers. It struck me how influential the Royal Family were outside the UK and that many Spanish followed their lives and indiscretions. Perhaps it mirrored their own?

The walk today was wooded; traditional oak to start our day and then plantations of eucalyptus with its pungent medicinal aroma accompanying our every breath. At least our tubes were clear. Forest walking is relaxing, paths are easy, the trees filter out the view ahead so that, despite the increasing numbers of people on the route, it seemed as if we were all alone. And then, as if by magic, we'd arrived at that night's stop.

Arzúa, the '*land of cheese, honey and philosophy*' a bright orange sign nailed to a tree informed us. Stark magnolia painted concrete apartment blocks were the reality and even the brightly coloured Miró mouse signage or kindergarten coloured bike racks could not detract from the post-modernist drabness.

"Is this all for us?" said I. Our apartment for the night was huge, newly decorated, although we were aware that there was always the possibility that we would be sharing. We took the biggest of the three bedrooms, made ourselves a state of the art pod machine coffee and clocked the brand new washing machine. Letting the place out to pilgrims would guarantee that it wouldn't look this pristine in a month or so's time.

A roadside square seemed a good bet for lunch. Lynne, being an ex civil servant, always worked on the theory of eating where the council workers ate, and this is where they were. Then at 2.00pm they all disappeared leaving us in peace again. Wolfgang and Elke strode by, their walking poles clacking like a metronome on the pavement with typical German efficiency. We arranged to meet them for a pre-dinner drink later in the day.

Whilst there was little to do in the town, we did have washing to attend to and as we padded naked backwards and forwards to the washer and drier, I was always just a little worried that someone else would be using the other two rooms. In fact, I did hear sounds that could have been a neighbour, but we never saw anyone.

Again, we were spoilt for choice for dinner but beforehand we met up with our German friends who said that their accommodation was terrible. We were able to tell them about how super ours was. As the sun shone, and we conversed over a beer or two, a pigeon flew over and deposited a present upon Wolfgang. I said that it was lucky in England and he said the Germans had a similar superstition.

We had a pleasant change for dinner in an Italian joint specialising in square pizzas washed down with another bottle of El Bierzo wine. We didn't avail ourselves of the board games on offer but did pop back to the main drag for a nightcap before retiring to bed.

Fresh fruit and cake were provided for breakfast and it was easy to forget that we were on the Camino, but to the path we had to go and we soon joined (mainly) Spanish pilgrims on this, the penultimate day of the route.

We ascertained that it was yet another national holiday and we heard singing from the churches that we passed. A fellow pilgrim explained that the event had started on the Saturday, although we never got to the bottom of what it was. Galicia Literature Day came up on an Internet search.

It wasn't long before we heard the tapping of the Blind Pew[1] Germans behind us and we passed an amicable few hours walking with Wolfgang and Elke; Wolfgang amusing us with his almost bottomless pit of very poor German jokes mistranslated into English.

We reached O' Pedrouzo at lunchtime and went in search of some protection from the sun, which came in the form of a stark 1980's night club with umbrellas outside providing shade to sturdy wooden benches. Of an evening the place was probably heaving with very drunk pilgrims, but at lunchtime it was quiet with the owner patiently doing her accounts on the next table.

It was another case of 'hunt the accommodation' and again we found that we were not staying at the place we thought we'd booked. The owner took us 200 metres down the road to the outskirts of the village where she showed us a small two bedroomed apartment overlooking fields and an amorous donkey. Actually, I was not sure why it was amorous as there was no lady donkey in the field. However, if one turned up he was more than ready to perform.

So close to Santiago and even the most commercial of restaurants were still providing a ten euro pilgrim menu. Today's offering was a Russian salad, spicy pork and runny cold custard. We sat with a couple of Spaniards and a girl from Ipanema (honestly). Don Quixote came up in conversation. The Spaniards had studied Cervantes at school although the only bit they could remember was the story about Sancho Panza and him being too frightened to go to the toilet. People never forget great literature.

In the distance we could hear the nightclub faintly throbbing and were drawn to it. This time there were groups of young people sitting in the warmth of the evening bathed in the light of hundreds of multicoloured bulbs. Whilst the locals may have been starting their evening, we were at the end of ours and settled for a Francesca hazelnut liqueur with our espressos. Note to self; avoid any nut based liqueur.

---

[1] A character in Treasure Island by Robert Louis Stevenson who would be heard tapping his white stick before he was seen.

The donkey was still in a state of readiness as we started on our last day of the Camino proper. We met up with our toilet reference companions from the previous night who were carrying ridiculously small rucksacks. "All mouth and no rucksack" as Lynne said, perhaps a little too loudly, as one of them stated that they had "cheated a little bit". If we met them in the Compostela queue we would dob them in.

By mid morning the thermometer in the café we had stopped at for a late breakfast showed 30°C. It was going to be another hot one.

A Radox[1] essence hit us as we walked through dense eucalyptus forest. The leaves cracking like gunshot as the sun dried them. The occasional aeroplane flew overhead and we soon circled the main airport for the city.

Considering we were no more than a dozen kilometres from our destination, the pilgrim traffic was light and we saw far fewer walkers than we had seen the previous days. Where were they? Were we lost?

Damien and Evelyn caught up with us. Evelyn was carrying a bunch of flowers Damien had given her for her birthday. Such a romantic. Impractical, but romantic. I remembered my birthday present to Lynne was a badge with Ibuprofen written on it. Perhaps not as romantic. We agreed to try and meet up when we got to Santiago and exchanged telephone numbers.

A stark concrete accommodation campus overlooked the city, its block houses reminiscent of a derelict concentration camp. It was here that we caught our first sight of the spires of the cathedral, a sight that many millions had done so previously for a thousand years.

Drab retail outlets selling second hand office furniture seemed to make up much of the light industrial permitted use of Santiago's suburbs. We could have been anywhere in the world and then we caught the sound of a discordant piper playing a lament in the air and following its mesmerising melody like Hamelin's kinder[2], we passed through an ancient stone arch to find ourselves at the Praza Obradoiro Catedral.

Clad in scaffolding and plastic sheeting our destination was, perhaps, a little deflating. I expected to be elated or perhaps sad that

---

[1] Famous for its bath salts since 1908 in the UK.
[2] The Pied Piper of Hamelin by Robert Browning. 'Kinder' – 'children' in German.

this was the end of the journey but I felt nothing. No sense of occasion. Lynne said she felt quite emotional but it may have been the pain and exhaustion.

I know others felt very differently and many had started their final steps at five in the morning to get here at noon for the church service. A service to venerate Saint James turning up to help a group of Christians kill some other people that were a bit different from them. Thank God for religion!

Scores of people milled about and we spotted a gaggle of German girls we had met the night before and we took it in turns to take each other's photos in front of the cathedral, our dusty walking boots firmly planted in the recessed shell marking the end of our journey.

The bagpipes still chanted (droned) on as we made our way to the hotel that we had booked for the night. The hotel that had allocated us a room overlooking the said bagpiper who played the same monotonous dirge over and over and over again.

The plan was now to spend a few days in Santiago and then decide whether to continue our journey west, to the end of the Roman earth. We had plenty of time to think about our plans and after splashing water on our faces, we went out to explore.

As we hit the pavement we met Damien and Evelyn again and arranged to meet up later at their hotel. We were heading for one of the craft beer bars that Santiago boasted but were disappointed to find that it was just about to close – well, it was lunchtime. We therefore sat at the café next door where, according to my diary, we had an 'interesting tapas that tasted of 1950s' damp bathroom'.

The plan had been to collect our certificate of completion, the Compostela and the distance certificate, but the queue snaked around the block and it was obviously going to be at least a couple of hours of standing in the sun – time much better spent drinking beer.

At the appointed time we rendezvoused with Damien and Evelyn. Well, Damien really as Evelyn had decided to go and bag a table at a nearby café and when we found her, she was working her way through a bucket of sangria. Having experienced the after effects of sangria before, I decided to plump for a beer. I was obviously going to be an amateur in the drinking stakes as Damien and Evelyn had already consumed a bottle of wine in the short time between our chance meeting at lunchtime and now.

Bar Two. More beer and more sangria, this time served in a large Kilner jar. Wolfgang and Elke joined us. Much toasting followed. A group of French came to the party. They told us that they were all retired SNCF workers and I regaled them with my story about trying to catch a train all those weeks ago when we had started the Camino. Whether it was the lack of contrition for the inconvenience I had suffered or the fact that they were only 56 years old and had retired a number of years earlier, I don't know, but Wolfgang practically exploded with indignation that he, a German, was probably paying for the French to retire at 50.

Our Spanish Cervantes experts passed by and recommended a restaurant around the corner. We needed food and all traipsed off and were seated in the restaurant with its pristine white tablecloths and up market menu. We all sat down and then got up again. This didn't feel right. What we really wanted was cheap wine and tapas and camaraderie and so we decamped to the bare melamine tables at the front of the bar for pork and potatoes, clams, scallops and chipirones (cuttlefish) and got comfortably numb on Rioja.

SANTIAGO DE COMPOSTELA – FINISTERRE

The city was just … far too city-like for us and after travelling across Spain with very few cares we were now saying things like "Make sure you hang on to your bag". A group of Romanians were scamming the more naïve pilgrims and it all felt a little unsafe. So, at 7.30am we got up and decided that we would set off to Finisterre – the end of the Earth.

We were also quite hungover.

We stopped for breakfast at an English style café that wouldn't have looked out of place in the Cotswolds. We also needed a bank but, as is often the case when desperate to find something, none were to be had.

Walking out of Santiago was a breath of fresh air, literally. Whereas the entrance had been through drab, tiresome suburbs the other side of the city boasted little in the way of buildings and we were soon walking through the Parque San Lorenzo. As we reached a peak, we looked back to see the Cathedral swathed in an ethereal mist. This would be the photo of the trip (see back cover).

As the heat rose, the mist lifted. It was going to be another lovely day. Again, we were surrounded by eucalyptus trees, their pungent scent guaranteeing clear nasal passages for all those walking the route. A Camino signpost afforded us the opportunity to go to Fisterra (Spanish spelling) or Muxía. Walking to Muxía would have been a lovely idea but even with us foregoing a couple of days in Santiago, we probably didn't have the time to do the round trip.

We were heading for the Alto de Vento; the clue was in the name and a friendly Italian gleefully told us that it was all up, and he was not wrong. "*Slow and tortuous*" I wrote in my diary, not helped by the fact that I had developed a blister. This was only the second blister of the entire trip, quite an achievement by any standards.

Any civilised country would have built a café at the top.

Ponte Maceira was God blessed. The local coat of arms described the intervention of the Almighty smiting the bridge to stop the Romans from slaughtering the followers of Saint James. God was a lot more smitier in those days. Next was Negreira, not a pretty town, and we came across a small hotel of the commercial traveller type. It was clean and functional. Then off for lunch of omelette and beer.

Returning to our hotel we rested however, on waking up, I found a black bug on the pillow. Bed Bug? Possibly. Personally, I had never seen one before and this one appeared to be dead. Searching the sheets, I found no other evidence of infestation and had certainly not been bitten and so was prepared to give the place the benefit of the doubt.

A bar promised pizza tapas, a selection of different pizzas, and it made a change. The homemade chorizo was especially delicious. We got talking to a few other pilgrims. We were now back in committed pilgrim territory rather than the plastic variety encountered over the past week or so. That sounds rather harsh, but there was certainly a difference between those that had spent weeks or months on the road and the Sarria pilgrims who had all the graces of day-trippers on a charabanc to Margate[1].

On waking, the first thing I checked for was bed bug bites. Luckily there were none and so to breakfast of bread, yoghurt and fruit with coffee you could stand a spoon up in. This would wake us up.

The Brierley guide, oh yes there was a separate guide for this stretch (again with '*Mystical Path*' notes: '*We generally experience death and dying as unwelcome visitors*' – too right we do!) suggested a 34km (21 miles) stretch. This was far too long so we decided to halve it.

With accommodation being somewhat less geared up for pilgrims and few albergues, we needed to find somewhere to sleep and so, over breakfast, we found a likely looking hotel a little off the beaten track. We e-mailed them and the proprietor e-mailed back to say he would pick us up from a local bar and to ring him when we arrived.

The day was damp and dreary and even though the terrain was pleasant enough (eucalyptus and oak again) the morning was a bit of a trudge, EU funded paths notwithstanding. The highlight of the morning? A signpost to a village that appeared to be called 'Porno'. Many a pilgrim had photographed that; us included.

---

[1] An old fashioned and often open topped bus used for trips to the seaside. Margate a seaside town on the south east coast 130 kilometres from London.

The Bar Casa Victoriano could have been transported directly from the Yorkshire Dales[1], along with taciturn landlord. When we asked if they did any food we were told "Eye, 'appen we do bocadillos" or the Spanish equivalent.

As we ordered our second beer we called the hotel and told them where we were. We expected to have a bit of time to drink our beer but, as if by magic, the hotel proprietor walked thought the door ready to whisk us away.

Now, we think of driverless cars as a modern concept. No. The avuncular Antonio had perfected the art of driving at breakneck speeds without touching the steering wheel, perhaps a light guiding nudge here and there, perhaps a little knee movement, but that was it. We had also made the schoolchild error of speaking a little basic Spanish to him. This resulted in Antonio having much to say to us throughout the entire 11 km journey making a point of looking at us directly in the eye, including Lynne who was in the back seat. We understood not a word. It was likely that a change of pants would be needed when we reached our destination.

The Hotel Rustico Santa Eulalia was in the middle of nowhere – and then a bit further on. 'Ancient' would describe it well although it had been well converted and rooms were spacious and comfortable with very, very thick walls. We even had our very own greenhouse outside the balcony door – perfect for drying damp pants – now clean.

Maria (Mrs Antonio) served us a pre-dinner beer and was extremely patient with our appalling Spanish, nodding and laughing in all the right places.

"[Something, something, something] Irish Times." Antonio was telling us about press cuttings mentioning the hotel. We nodded and we too laughed in all the right places. Quid pro quo.

Antonio's uncle was a painter, not of the 'and decorator' variety, but of the easel and jaunty beret school. When we had run out of paintings on the walls we could then appreciate even more of them in a coffee table book. We needed feeding.

---

[1] Range of large hills in northern England.

We were joined by a German and Australian couple, both of them new blood for the Irish Times story and guided gallery tour. Once seated we took what came as there was no menu. I was provided with a steak whilst Lynne had grilled chicken. I think they must have sized us up and decided what we were most likely to eat. We were more than happy with this. A very fresh tuna salad accompanied the meat and we washed it down with a Rectoral de Amandi Mencía. I was somewhat concerned that this might have something to do with bottoms. However, the back of the bottle described the wine as having *'soft touches of tannin providing a persistent finish that invites to continue disgusting'*! It wasn't disgusting, it was quite nice.

Our underwear had crisped up nicely on the balcony. Breakfast was laid out in the dining room: eggs, cured meats, cheese bread, yoghurt – a feast fit for a pilgrim. We did what everyone else seems to have done and made a breakfast sandwich.

Another trip in the semi-autonomous Mercedes which had been programmed to stop at some ancient standing stones (Dolmen Perxubeira) close to the path. We thanked Antonio and set out in the drizzle to look at a muddy field with a couple of flat stones in the middle. Perhaps we weren't cut out to be archaeologists.

We walked back to our start point in the drizzle only to be told off on the way by a woman who told us that we shouldn't be walking by the side of the road as it was dangerous. As if we had a choice.

More inspiring guidance from Mr Brierley, this time informing me that without spirituality in my life I was only travelling down a cul-de-sac of despair with a nasty death awaiting me at the end. Thanks John!

We now had a reasonably short eight miles to cover for the day, meeting up with Australians and Mexicans who we had walked with before. The Mexican ladies were kind enough to share their nuts with us and in no time at all we had reached our destination, Olveiroa.

Our accommodation was As Pias, a rural gastropub (if the Spanish have such a thing), with thick, rustic sone walls and large windows. My diary entry says they were very 'clued up'. I'm not sure what I meant. Perhaps they were not shy in charging. As we walked in, we poked our noses into the kitchen with its table laden with chicken, crab and octopus. We would eat well tonight.

It occurred to us how disparate the villages we passed through were. Some villages were practically derelict with little population to talk of and, perhaps, one poor café with a few nondescript rooms. Others like Olveiroa were buzzing with a number of pleasant, up market bars, restaurants and hostals. Nothing appeared to be different in location – they were all on a linear path – but some prospered whilst others died.

We popped into the bar up the road for a beer and a toasted sandwich while watching the Spanish rioting on the news. The Spanish were always protesting about something and today's gripe was about pensions. Something about the Germans not subsidising early retirement for Spanish transport workers probably. After a perusal of the evening menu we decided to eat back in our accommodation later on.

We were confused about the lack of crab and octopus, they weren't on the menu. A mystery, but other than that we ate well. After dinner, we returned to our lunchtime haunt, and got talking to Toni, a vision mixer for TV who appeared to be on a year-long sabbatical. We thought he said that he was being paid for it – good luck to him. We sat drinking beer watching a very sub-standard Liverpool play an on the ball Real Madrid. Neither of us were particularly interested in the football; Toni was a Barcelona fan and I had no interest in the game at all. Not something you readily admit to in a bar in Spain.

Toni, it turned out, was a babe magnet. As soon as we took our eyes off him, he would be schmoozing the fairer sex; this time Molly, an American pilgrim and Monica, half Galician and half Colombian – a very good mix of genes.

Real Madrid won 3-1.

Now we knew where the octopus and crab went. We got back to our room at elevenish and once in bed were immediately regaled by a second tranche of guests who drank, ate and talked loudly until two in the morning. Had we not have been quite so knackered and full of beer from drinking with Toni, we might have joined in or at least complained.

We ate breakfast with a couple of locals who had a large gin and tonic and some sort of green liqueur with their croissants. These were remnants from last night's party. You had to admire these Spaniards' stamina.

Big food was not an option when rucksack space was at a premium. The bocadillos from the café at O' Casteliño were a half a metre in length and wouldn't fit into the rucksack. We considered duct taping them to the top of the bag, but that would have involved unpacking everything. We knew that we would be unable to eat them all, so ditching half of them would have been the logical thing to do. But, hey, when do logic and cheese mix?

A kilometre further and we were at Cruce and another opportunity to divert off to Muxía if we wanted. This was still a possibility but would have involved some hard and fast walking and we both rather fancied having a relaxing couple of days at the end of the Earth, so we headed left to Finisterre. This was a required photo opportunity, leaning on the dual direction markers.

By the marker we found another packed lunch, obviously forgotten by photogenic pilgrims like us stopping off for a snap. Like the good Samaritans that we were, we decided to take it with us and find the forgetful owner. We now had three large lunches. As we passed slower walkers, we quizzed them but, no takers.

"Perhaps they were going to Muxía?" One helpful traveller suggested. We hadn't thought of that, now some poor soul, noticing that they had left their lunch behind, would retrace their steps to find their food snaffled.

The spewing chimneys of the carbide factory dominated the skyline for a bit, but soon serenity was restored and we lunched at a beautiful little chapel in a field, Ermita de San Pedro Mártir. This would have made a lovely wild camping spot had we not have been able to get to Cee and we remarked that, to date, we had been remarkably lucky in finding accommodation wherever we had stopped for the night. We ate half of one of the bocodillos and a banana from the stolen lunch pack we had picked up.

We dipped our boots into a little stream as it advertised being a cure for sore feet, before descending the last five kilometres to Cee. And there it was, the Atlantic, our first sight of the coast.

We dumped our bags at our hotel – note 'hotel' not 'hostal' (we were moving up in the world), and we were drawn inexorably towards the sea. Busy market stalls were selling everything from food to clothes to ironmongery. We bumped into Toni.

"Follow me". We followed and Toni took us on a gastronomic tour of the artisan food stalls. Chewy rustic rye breads, spicy dried sausages and queso tetilla, a Galician cows' milk cheese so named as it resembles a small breast and nipple. We really felt like locals and as a thank you to Toni, offered to buy him lunch.

I'm not sure the 6% half litres of 1909 beer was a particularly good idea, but the tapas was lovely: Russian salad, chickpeas in rich tomato and paprika sauce, pork and sausage in a sweet piquant sauce, all supplied free with our beers. We felt obliged to have quite a few of them as we had quite a debt to repay Toni! We then bade him goodbye as he was hoping to make Finisterre that night.

The seaside plaza, with its formal lawns and promenades enabled us to walk off our beer ready for the next part of the day with more eating and drinking planned. Peter, he of the octopus evening, called out to us and we sat with him over a beer, promising to meet up later.

The pizzas we found for dinner were doing a grand job of soaking up the alcohol we had drunk during the day, but things were just about to get far messier.

On the way back to the hotel we came across a lively locals' bar with rowdy but amiable customers conversing and arguing. The sensible thing to have done would have been to carry on walking. Not ones to be sensible, we strolled in. We stood at the bar, soaking up the atmosphere, Some Spanish chap engaged us in conversation. Perhaps the use of the word 'conversation' was a bit stretched. We spoke our few words of Spanish to him and he gabbled back, neither of us understanding the other. We bought him a drink. He bought us one back. My diary says; 'Difficult to remember much more'.

This was to be our very last day of walking. I was feeling rather slow but did have a vague memory of buying cheese and ham to feed the café cat the night before. The breakfast coffee and churros were much needed.

This last, and very short, leg took us through coastal villages with spectacular views of the Atlantic from quaint and deserted little coves. We could smell the ozone. This felt more like the fitting end to our walk that we had hoped for. And then, there it was; the end of the Earth.

A ramshackle beach café supplied us with fuel to walk across the kilometre long beach into town. Seagulls hopped about our feet, occasionally waves forced us to tango away from the water's edge, this was the perfect overture to the finale of our journey – perhaps a metaphor too far?

Tables and chairs graced the waterfront pavements. We needed to celebrate, we needed that perfect beer. The waiter arrived with a couple of pintas and a menu. We plumped for a rich and spicy fish soup, a bowl of steamed mussels, squid in its own ink and paella. The menu came with a bottle of cheap white plonk. It could have been the best white burgundy, it was perfect – idyllic. The waiter took a photo. The inane grin said it all.

A group of Americans and Colombians sat next to us. Elizabeth ("named after your Queen") was very garrulous and told us her life story. We had nothing better to do, so we listened, smiled, nodded.

Toni walked by. He would have stopped for a drink but was too engaged with two women who were hanging on his every word. This man exuded pheromones by the bucketload.

The lunchtime diners slowly dispersed and we did too. Back at our hotel we went through the ritual of discarding our dirty walking clothes and donned our (only just) cleaner clothes. This would be the last time I would rinse out my lurid yellow, orange and green underpants; the ones I had chosen so they would stand out on any communal washing line.

The hum of people having a relaxing time greeted us back at the harbour front. Early evening sun gave a creamy whiteness to the scene. Glasses clinked. Chairs scraped.

"Are you on your own?"

"May I join you?"

"Good to see you again."

Pilgrims greeted each other. Old friends caught up. New friendships were made.

Lynne and I would miss this simplistic lifestyle. We'd lived out of a 35 litre rucksack for two months. Everything we needed we had carried: clothes, a sleeping bag, toiletries, a towel, walnuts… Tomorrow we would dispense with anything we didn't need for the journey home and finally eat the nuts.

In a side street a 'nano' bar caught our attention. Three stools at a bar with no legroom. This looked uncomfortable and inconvenient. We went in. The 'Bastard Bitter' was fine. Very English. Upstairs there was an equally minuscule restaurant. A cubby hole became vacant and we squeezed in, being careful not to move the chair too far back lest it toppled (with me) down a spiral staircase.

We perused the menu. I wasn't sure about the '*spider crap pâté*', not being sure how much crap a spider did. So, I went for the homemade hummus followed by local Galician hamburger in an artisan roll with padron pepper marmalade. All very Hoxton[1] with a bearded hipster waiter to boot.

My hi-vis underwear was still a little damp, but that didn't matter as we had the luxury of a two night stay. One of the most useful pieces of equipment I had brought with me had been the bit of string that had come out day after day as our washing line. And, of course, we now had our Camino pegs from Vega de Valcarce.

"Are you ready to order or would you like a couple more minutes?" said our waitress at the bar we'd chosen for breakfast. This was politeness and efficiency unknown in most of the cafés we'd encountered along the route. Needless to say, the place was run by Germans. Whilst we loved the sometimes chaotic and laid back approach of the Spanish serving staff, it was really nice to have some Nordic order and proficiency. Having said that, our uber-efficient waitress gave us the wrong bill.

Whilst we had reached Finisterre we were still not quite at the end of the Earth. That terminus awaited us three kilometres further west. We walked slowly, rather like not wanting to finish a good novel, savouring every last step. Purple, tie-dyed, harem-panted hippies joined us along the way and I very nearly decided to give it all up and join them in their rejection of all things conventional.

The lighthouse, our destination and of countless others, came into sight and we walked towards the beacon, passing the 0.000KM way-marker. We had made it.

The waves broke upon the rocks with the rhythmic regularity of rushes on a tight drum. Other than that, it was silent. We had left the beatniks and the 'flowers in their hair' beautiful people behind somewhere and just a handful of pilgrims sat on the rocks after dipping their boots into the sea. Little piles of ash could be found in the crevices where people had cremated their boots and a gigantic bronze boot statue represented, as much as the shell, the 600 miles, 900 kilometres that we had all walked to get here.

---

[1] Trendy area of north east London.

154

There was an end of the world feel to the place; the sort of landscape that you get in Cornwall or Western Ireland. A coastline constantly battered by Atlantic storms, not pretty but wild and rugged.

A lone bagpiper turned up. Standing in his blue checked shirt, silhouetted against the pale blue of the sky, he played a Gallic lament. Money, as they say, may have been able to buy most things (love?) but that particular moment in time was priceless. So, we sat, listening to the pipes, the sea, the gulls and were at peace with the world. We had purposefully arrived early and my suspicion about the place filling up was confirmed as more and more sightseers descended on the site. However, I had had my moment of calm and tranquillity and was now ready for a coffee. We bumped into Peter from Alabama and arranged to meet later.

Leaving via the road I saw the size of the car park. The souvenir shops were just opening for the day and we could see that later the place would be heaving with flip flop wearing tourists. I remembered a line from a David Bowie song; *"See the mice in their million hordes, From Ibiza to the Norfolk Broads"*. We pilgrims were not mice; we were giants among men (and women).

Our preferred choice of restaurant for lunch was inconveniently closed (we were looking forward to the 35 euro tasting menu) and then we found that all the restaurants closed on a Tuesday. You would have thought that they would have staggered this, given that it was a tourist destination.

We met up with Peter and found an open restaurant for lunch: scallops, squid, garlic prawns, padron peppers and a bottle of

Albariño. Peter told us that he had been scattering sand from home. "So much lighter than a pebble" he said. The owner brought three very green liqueurs to finish off our meal.

With all this zen calmness, the opportunity to have one final fling presented itself in the form of a boat offering cruises around the headland and with little better to do we jumped on board. A large group of Spanish pilgrims were already on board and had obviously started their celebrating early. It appears that the conga is universal.

That evening Peter joined us for a nightcap brandy and we reminisced about our favourite places along the route and laughed about the people we had met and miserable days in the rain. And so, we bade farewell to Peter, knowing that we were very unlikely to ever meet again. That was the way of the Way; passing ships and fleeting friendships and very long memories.

We caught the bus back to Santiago. The timetable said 14.20 the bus arrived at 13.20 and we were lucky to be in the vicinity when it turned up. It was funny being in a vehicle again after 50 days of walking. I can't say I enjoyed it very much.

Santiago was grey and uninviting. However, we had a mission; to get our Compostela. The queue wasn't quite as long as it had been on our previous visit and we joined it, slowly snaking towards one of the counters to have our passports checked as proof we had walked the whole route. I was asked why I had walked it and given a list of responses. I said "spiritual" as did most of the pilgrims that I saw listed on the spreadsheet in front of my volunteer clerk. There was a reason for this; anything other than walking for 'religious' or ''spiritual' reasons meant receiving a Certificado rather than a Compostela and, if you had walked 800 kilometres you wanted something unreadable in Latin to say you'd done it.

In celebration, we visited a craft beer bar and spoilt ourselves with a pineapple IPA, smoky chipotle IPA and a maple stout (7.2%). For anyone who is not a beer lover, these probably sound disgusting but I thought they were heavenly. I tried to text Raymond and Barbara to say we had finished but the text would not go through, so I phoned them. As I've said before, it's funny the relationships that people form on the Camino.

We'd arranged to meet Wolfgang and Elke in the evening and shared a steaming paella with them in the posh part of the restaurant we'd visited the previous week. Somehow this felt better than last time when we'd asked to be moved. My diary says that it *'was a very pleasant night, if not a bit Teutonic'*.

We laid in. Well, managed to stay in bed until 7.45am which was late for us. Time to shop for some tat. If it's tat you want then Roman Catholicism is up there with Blackpool Beach[1] for tacky gifts. I once picked up a luminous plastic bottle of holy water in the shape of the Virgin Mary in Fatima, Portugal and even I was offended.

We had strenuously avoided buying anything along the route, well, at least anything that weighed anything more than a few grams. Now I was free to pick up a souvenir or two, as long as it fitted into the rucksack. My first must was a 'been there, done that' tee shirt and mug to remind me of the trip on a daily basis. The only problem was it was still the crack of dawn.

Santiago is not just about tourists and pilgrims, it's a working city as well, and once out of the cathedral area a functioning busy metropolis awaited. Our research suggested that the Café Derby was worth a visit and one of the oldest establishments in the city.

Steeped in tradition and antiquity, the dark wood panelled bar opened its doors in 1929 and had seen countless writers, bohemians and intellectuals discussing the issues of the day. The only thing missing was a fog of cigarette smoke and a bronze statue of Ernest Hemingway. We ordered coffee and admired the Fin de Époque marble counter and the green topped tables. It was fussy and the waiters aloof but after the buzz of the tourist area it felt like a soft leather sofa – comfy and protective. Unfortunately, when conducting research for this book, I was disheartened to learn that the Derby had closed its doors permanently after 92 years.

---

[1] Holiday resort in the north west of England.

157

After seven weeks of walking, this last day was a bit of a novelty if not somewhat unstructured. It was also dawning on me that this was the conclusion of the adventure and that tomorrow we would re-enter the real world and to this end, we went to find the bus stop and suss out timings for our return journey.

The souvenir shops were many and the choice of rubbish boundless, but I managed to pick up my tee shirt and mug together with a Camino shell ceramic tile for the garden at home. By this time, we had wasted enough time for it to be lunchtime and headed for the Rúa do Franco, the main thoroughfare and tapas strip.

We were looking for that archetypal brown wooded, bay-windowed establishment with white aproned waiters busily running between tables, trays held high on bended elbows. And there it was. We secured seats at the counter with its vast array of dishes. We pointed and asked what things were and were entertained by the waiter constantly annoying the razor clams who popped in and out of their shells. In the end we settled for a selection of albondigas, cuttlefish, prawns and croquetas, all perfectly Spanish.

Full of beer and tapas we headed for the cathedral to pay homage to Saint James himself. What we found was a mass of polythene and scaffolding. Saint James was having a makeover.

Being unreligious I find the 'bling' of these churches quite offensive. The amount of money spent on decorating them, money that had, no doubt, come from the poor members of society, perhaps would better have been spent on those poor themselves.

We joined a queue; well, we are British. This was the queue to see the supposed bones of St. James, the man who had inspired our life for the last couple of months. I was reminded of the Pardoner in Chaucer's *Canterbury Tales*[1]: '*He hadde a croys of latoun ful of stones, And in a glas he hadde pigges bones.*'

Whilst all was quiet today, the Cathedral is busiest for the pilgrims' mass and especially when the Botafumeiro is set a swinging. This is a dirty great big perfume ball, full of charcoal and incense which is swung from one end of the cathedral to the other on a rope hauled by

---

[1] Early English text containing 24 stories told on a pilgrimage from London to Canterbury (Kent – south east England).

eight hunky tiraboleiros (red robed church officials) at 80 kilometres an hour. Whether the smoke keeps the devil away, is for purification and sanctification or to mask the foul odour of past unwashed pilgrims, I knew not.

Any museum filled with religious artifacts always strikes me along the same lines as visiting a Harry Potter theme park. All very interesting and all that, but ultimately, we're just looking at stuff that's made up. Of more interest is why people believe in all of it, but that's a discussion for another day.

The brand new Museum of Pilgrimage and Santiago never addressed any of the fundamental questions about why people went on pilgrimage although I did glean one interesting fact: the verb 'to roam' comes from the pilgrims going to Rome. I added this to my 'saunter' knowledge.

Our last night and plenty of bars to visit. The Cervexería Xuntanza served a very interesting mushroom beer. I say 'interesting' as it was sort of a cross between Marmite[1] and a beef stock cube. I wouldn't be having it again.

We finished off our evening with the traditional coffee and Spanish brandy. We found a little locals' bar away from the tourists and sat at our melamine table on plastic chairs in quiet contemplation of all that had happened over the last, nearly two months.

We had met so many people, some who had become friends. We had suffered with them, laughed with them and had some significant hangovers with them. We had a diary full of scribbled (and sometimes illegible) thoughts, a camera full of photos and a head (and heart) full of memories. And most of all we had a sense of achievement. Many people thought, and still think today, that walking 900 kilometres across Spain is madness. Perhaps it was but I wouldn't have missed it for the world.

"Lynne ...?"
"Yes" she said.

---

[1] Savoury yeast spread.

HOME

When we arrived home our elderly neighbour had pinned a hand drawn 'welcome home' to the door and so we put down our rucksacks on the kitchen floor and felt depressed.

Piles of post were, well, piled up on the kitchen counter for us, 90 percent going straight into the recycling bin. There were no writs, which was a good thing and we'd pre paid our credit card bill so that wasn't an issue. In fact, we'd hopelessly over budgeted for our trip … when have you ever heard someone say that? Accommodation was cheap, food even cheaper and with a Spanish brandy at a euro or so a bucket it had proved difficult to drink the budget (or satisfy the Spanish chief medical officer's recommendation) either.

Now for SNCF. I rang their help line and spoke with a gentleman who, whilst not speaking much English (and me speaking atrocious French) was willing to battle through the conversation.

"Monsieur, j'ai acheté un billet pour la SNCF mais il n'est pas allé parce que vous étiez en une grève."

"Quand avez-vous acheté le billet ?"

"Il y a 53 jours."

"Je suis désolé, mais le maximum est de 50 jours. L'ordinateur dit 'non'"

The gist of this is that refunds have to be claimed within 50 days and we were out of the country for more than that (by three days)…

SNCF – bless them!

OUR FRIENDS

Many people exchange names and addresses when they meet people on holiday. Most of these are forgotten or, even worse, that loud couple with the appalling taste in beachwear search you out for an excruciating evening of holiday slides and atrocious wine.

However, the Camino was different. Lasting friendships were formed over very short periods of time. I am not sure why this was. Perhaps it was the sheer scale of the trip, the pain we suffered together, the dormitories full of snoring travellers? I know not, but good friends were made all the same.

Wolfgang and Elke (Swabian Albs, Germany)

These lovely people came to stay with us in Somerset in the autumn of 2018. Wolfgang's brother had been born here when his father was a prisoner of war (PoW), held in Taunton, Somerset. His father had been captured and initially held by the Italians who, being Italian, were somewhat chaotic in their administration of PoWs. Some of the Germans were then taken by the Russians, others came to England to a 300 PoW camp at Cross Keys, Norton Fitzwarren, Somerset. These prisoners worked on local farms and, being low risk, appeared to have many freedoms to come and go as they pleased. Researching this for

Wolfgang, we found to our upmost surprise that part of the camp still existed and the Nissen huts were still there.

This year (2022) we made it to Germany and stayed with them. We were looked after royally – if not fed a little too much cake!

Peter (Dublin, Ireland)

In February 2019 we jumped on a plane to Ireland to meet up with Peter.

We spent a fantastic couple of days on a very long pub crawl around some of Dublin's most interesting bars.

During the Covid lockdown we had virtual drinks with Peter on a number of occasions and hope to see him at the launch of this book.

Evelyn and Damien (Dublin, Ireland)

At the same time as visiting Peter we also met up with Evelyn and Damien (who I always want to call Brendan for some reason). A great evening took place with much laughter and reminiscing.

Barbara and Raymond (Eversdal, South Africa)

Being in South Africa it is a bit more difficult to hop on a plane for the weekend. However, we have kept in touch by e-mail since. Barbara kept up her pilgrimage experiences, completing the Tankwa Camino (259kms) in ten days through a part of the Karoo desert.

Peter (Alabama, USA)

Peter has undertaken the Camino a further two more times. In March 2019 we took three months off to hire a campervan and travel across the USA. We tried to get hold of Peter but without success, although stayed just a few miles from him at Gulf Shores in Alabama. We will catch up with him sometime.

THANK YOUS

I would like to thank the following people who helped to bring this book to publication:

Lynne who (secretly) enjoyed the walk as much as I did and read and re-read drafts of this book countless times. I occasionally suggest trying one of the other routes to Santiago… perhaps one day.

Peter Barton is my oldest friend and made many excellent comments and suggestions on the proof copy of the book. He was also very good at spotting the numerous 'auto correct' blunders during the typing process.

John Graham, a fluent French and Spanish speaker, proof read the final version of the book and was appalled at some of my spelling and grammatical mistakes. He also taught me the correct use of the Oxford comma, which I have mainly ignored!

Angela Lees is my most brutal proof reader and I am always terrified to get a proof copy back in the post from her.